Colorado Rules of
Evidence with Objections

Sixth Edition

Colorado Rules of Evidence with Objections

Sixth Edition

William G. Meyer
District Court Judge (Ret.)

Anthony J. Bocchino
Professor Emeritus
Temple University Beasley School of Law

David A. Sonenshein
Professor Emeritus
Temple University Beasley School of Law

NATIONAL INSTITUTE FOR TRIAL ADVOCACY

Address inquiries to:
Reprint Permission
National Institute for Trial Advocacy
1685 38th Street, Suite 200
Boulder, CO 80301-2735
Phone: (800) 225-6482
Email: permissions@nita.org

Official co-publisher of NITA.
WKLegaledu.com/NITA

ISBN 978-1-60156-884-7
FBA 1884

SUSTAINABLE FORESTRY INITIATIVE   Certified Sourcing   www.sfiprogram.org   SFI-01051

eISBN 978-1-60156-885-4
eISBN 1885

Library of Congress Cataloging-in-Publication Data

Names: Meyer, William G., author. | Bocchino, Anthony J., author. |
   Sonenshein, David A., author.
Title: Colorado rules of evidence with objections / William G. Meyer,
   District Court Judge (Ret.); Anthony J. Bocchino, Professor Emeritus,
   Temple University Beasley School of Law; David A. Sonenshein, Professor
   Emeritus, Temple University Beasley School of Law.
Description: Sixth edition. | Boulder, CO : National Institute for Trial
   Advocacy, [2020] | Summary: "Colorado Rules of Evidence, as amended to
   January 1, 2020, with objections and analysis"— Provided by publisher.
Identifiers: LCCN 2020008073 (print) | LCCN 2020008074 (ebook) | ISBN
   9781601568847 (spiral bound) | ISBN 9781601568854 (ebook)
Subjects: LCSH: Evidence (Law)—Colorado. | Court rules—Colorado.
Classification: LCC KFC2340 .M49 2020 (print) | LCC KFC2340
   (ebook) | DDC 347.788/06—dc23
LC record available at https://lccn.loc.gov/2020008073
LC ebook record available at https://lccn.loc.gov/2020008074

Printed in the United States.

Dedication

To Brooke Wunnicke, my mentor.
To Brenda Rivers, my soulmate and wife.
To Kristina and Britt,
our talented daughters.
To Ryan Ava Robinson,
our granddaughter, who continually fills a
place in our heart we didn't realize existed.

W.G.M.

PREFACE

This text is designed to provide the practitioner and student with a convenient reference for raising trial objections and presenting responses. This pocket-sized reference book affords the reader the opportunity to instantly consult the relevant section of the Colorado Rules of Evidence, which are reproduced in their entirety in the last section of the book.

The material is presented in alphabetical order; tabs are located on the edges of the pages to aid in locating the appropriate section. Responses are found on the same pages or sections as the objections.

The cross-reference to the applicable Colorado Rule(s) follows the objections and responses, and explanatory paragraphs conclude each topic. This explanatory segment is designed to alert the reader to a practice tip or legal interpretation crucial to proper understanding of the subject matter of that section.

This book is not designed to provide an in-depth analysis of evidentiary rulings or the application of the theories concerning the admission or exclusion of evidence. Instead, *Colorado Rules of Evidence with Objections* was developed to furnish readers with a complete reference of trial objections and responses and is small enough to be easily carried to the courtroom or the classroom. We hope you find this material assists you in the pursuit of improving your litigation skills.

CONTENTS

AMBIGUOUS QUESTIONS

Objection

• *I object on the grounds that the question is* (ambiguous—vague—unintelligible).

Response

• In most circumstances, it is better to rephrase the question unless counsel is certain of the question's clarity.

Cross-Reference to Colorado Rule

There is no Colorado Rule specifically covering forms of questions. The court has discretion to sustain the objection pursuant to Rule 611(a).

Explanation

An ambiguous question is one that is susceptible to at least two interpretations, or that is so vague or unintelligible as to make it likely to confuse the jury or witness.

ARGUMENTATIVE QUESTIONS

Objections

• *I object. The question is argumentative.*

• *I object. Counsel is arguing to the jury.*

Response

• *I am attempting to elicit evidence from the witness.*

Cross-Reference to Colorado Rule

There is no Colorado Rule specifically covering forms of questions. The court has complete discretion to sustain the objection pursuant to Rule 611(a) to protect witnesses from harassment.

Explanation

An argumentative question is one which does not seek information from the witness but rather, makes an argument to the jury in the guise of a question.

The objection to an argumentative question is not intended to cover the situation where the questioning counsel is arguing with the witness; rather, it applies to the situation where counsel comments on the evidence or attempts to draw inferences from the evidence thereby seeking the witness's response to such comments. It is jury argument in the guise of a question.

ASKED AND ANSWERED QUESTIONS

Objections

- *I object. That question has been asked and answered.*
- *I object. The witness has already answered the question.*

Responses

- *Opposing counsel is incorrect. The witness has not yet answered the question.*
- *The question has not been answered during my examination.*

Cross-Reference to Colorado Rule

There is no Colorado Rule specifically covering forms of questions. The court has discretion to sustain the objection pursuant to Rule 611(a), because the evidence is cumulative. Additionally, the objection may be sustained pursuant to Rule 403.

Explanation

A question may be objected to as "asked and answered" when it calls for the repetition of testimony from a witness who has previously given the same testimony in response to a question asked by examining counsel. It is designed to prevent cumulative evidence through repetition of testimony. *People In the Interest of E.G.*, 371 P.3d 693 (2015) (court excluded further inquiry as a "needless consumption of time" and as "cumulative").

ASSUMING FACTS NOT IN EVIDENCE

Objection

• *I object. The question assumes a fact not in evidence. There has been no testimony that* (insert facts that have been assumed).

Responses

• *I will elicit that fact from the witness in a separate question.*

• *That fact has been proved during the earlier testimony of this witness.*

• *That fact has been proved during the testimony of* (insert the name of another witness who has already testified).

• *This fact will be testified to during the testimony of* (insert the name of another witness who will testify later).

Cross-Reference to Colorado Rule

There is no Colorado Rule specifically covering forms of questions. The court has discretion to sustain the objection pursuant to Rule 611(a).

Explanation

A direct examination question is objectionable if it assumes, in the asking, facts that have not already been proved. These questions are another form of leading questions and are referred to as "misleading" questions. However, the trial court has discretion to depart from the usual order of presentation of evidence when necessary. *See* CRE 104(b); *People v. Lyle*, 613 P.2d 896 (Colo. 1980).

AUTHENTICATION OF INSTRUMENTS

Objection

• *I object. This exhibit has not been authenticated.*

Responses

• *This instrument has been authenticated by stipulation of counsel.*

• *The instrument has been authenticated by the testimony of* (insert name of witness who has testified) *that:*

» *the witness created the writing,* or

» *the witness was present when the writing was created and testified that it was in the same basic condition as at the time of its creation,* or

» *the witness knows the handwriting because he* (she) *saw the author write or sign the instrument,* or

» *the witness knows the handwriting from having seen the author sign at another time,* or

» *the witness knows the handwriting based upon familiarity not acquired for the purpose of litigation and by circumstantial evidence* (state such circumstantial evidence), or

› (where document is proved by an expert witness) *the expert has compared the handwriting in question with an authentic handwriting exemplar and that the expert's opinion to a reasonable degree of certainty is that the handwriting in question is that of* (insert name of purported author), or

› *the witness saw the scene or items portrayed in the photograph at a relevant time and that the photograph is a fair and accurate representation of what he* (she) *saw,* or

› *the witness can identify the record as a public document because the witness works at the agency where the record was recorded, filed, and/or kept and the law authorizes such recordation or filing,* or

› *the witness can identify the ancient document because 1) there are no suspicions about its authenticity, or 2) was found in a place where such ancient documents are kept, or 3) has been in existence more than twenty years,* or

› (for computer-generated documents, as opposed to computer-stored data) *the witness has authenticated the process or system by testifying about his* (her) *familiarity with the system or process and the results contained in the document are accurate.*

• *I request the court compare the handwriting in question with an admittedly authentic handwriting exemplar and find that it is the handwriting of* (insert name of purported author).

Cross-Reference to Colorado Rule 901

Authentication requires that the proponent establish that the item is what it purports to be. *People v. Warrick,* 284 P.3d 139 (Colo. App. 2011). In civil cases, counsel must object to the authenticity of trial exhibits twenty-eight days prior to trial as part of the proposed trial management order or the objection may be deemed to be waived. Rule 16(f)(3)(VI)(B), Colorado Rules of Civil Procedure.

Social media correspondence presents special problems in authentication because of the ease with which one can assume another's identity on such platforms as Facebook. *People in Interest of A.C.E-D.,* 2018 COA 157, ¶ 46. Social media communications require two showings for authentication: (1) the records were those of the social media platform, and (2) the communications recorded therein were authored by the person against whom they are offered. *State v. Dominguez-Castor,* 2020 COA 1. Other cases addressing authentication requirements include *People v. Heisler,* 2017 COA 58, ¶¶ 15–23 (text messages); *People v. Glover,* 2015 COA 16, ¶¶ 21–34 (Facebook messages); *People v. Bernard,* 2013 COA 79, ¶¶ 7–13 (emails); *People v. NTB,* 2019 COA 150 (cloud-based files like Dropbox); *People in Interest of MV,* 432 P.3d 628 (Colo. App. 2018) (video recordings).

Explanation

Unless an instrument is self-authenticating under Rule 902, its proponent must establish its identity and authorship before it can be accepted into evidence. The proponent of an instrument can fulfill the requirements of Rule 901 in a variety of ways, including stipulation, circumstantial evidence, or the testimony of a witness with knowledge of its identity and authorship. *People v. Gilmore*, 97 P.3d 123 (Colo. App. 2003). The court can also conditionally admit the document under Rule 104(b) and let the jury determine the issue of authentication. *People v. Crespi*, 155 P.3d 570 (Colo. App. 2006).

AUTHENTICATION OF TELEPHONE CONVERSATION AND VOICES

Objections

- *I object. The telephone conversation has not been authenticated.*

- *I object. The participants in the telephone conversation have not been properly identified.*

Responses

- *The identity of the participants in the telephone conversation has been established through the testimony of* (insert name of witness) *who has testified that:*

  » *the witness is familiar with and recognized the voice,* or

  » *the witness called the number listed to* (insert name of participant) *and the other party identified himself* (herself) *as* (insert name of participant), or

  » *the witness called the number listed to* (insert name of participant) *and the other party identified himself* (herself) *as* (insert name of participant), or

  » *the witness called the number listed to* (insert name of participant) *and the content of the conversation showed* (insert name of person) *to be the person who answered the call,* or

  » *the witness called the number listed to* (insert name of business) *and the conversation related to business conducted by* (insert name of business) *over the telephone,* or

» (where proof is established by expert witness testimony) *the expert has compared the voice in question with an authentic voice exemplar and that the expert's opinion to a reasonable degree of certainty is that the voice in question is that of* (insert name of purported speaker).

Cross-Reference to Colorado Rule 901

Colorado follows the federal rule regarding authentication of telephone conversations. However, in civil cases, Colorado allows testimony by telephone, when the interests of justice so require. The procedure for requesting evidence to be presented by telephone and the factors needed for admission are contained in Rule 43(i) of the Colorado Rules of Civil Procedure.

Explanation

Authentication of telephone conversations and voices is the process of proving the identity of the persons involved in the conversation. Before testimony can be had that a telephone conversation occurred, testimony must be elicited to prove the identity of the participants in the conversation. *People v. Czemerynski,* 786 P.2d 1100 (Colo. 1990). The court may require a witness to appear personally and testify in person, instead of by video conference. *People v. Casias*, 2012 COA 117.

An audio recording may be authenticated in various ways, as long as the proponent establishes that it is what it is represented to be. *People v. Gonzales*, 2019 COA 30 (rejecting the formulaic approach of *People v. Baca*, 2015 COA 153, but approving an extended analysis when there is a colorable claim that a recording has been altered, and suggesting the factors discussed in *Baca* may be highly pertinent to the authenticity determination); *People in Interest of MV*, 432 P. 3d 628 (Colo. App. 2018) (video recordings).

CHARACTER EVIDENCE: GENERALLY

Objection

• *The question calls for evidence of character on propensity.*

Response

• *This evidence is offered:*
  » *on propensity pursuant to Rule 404(a)(1) or 404(a)(2) through opinion or reputation evidence,* or
  » *for a relevant non-propensity purpose pursuant to Rule 404(b),* or
  » *to prove propensity where character is an essential element of a claim, charge, or defense pursuant to Rule 405(b).*

Cross-Reference to Colorado Rules 404 and 405

In a criminal case only, opinion and reputation evidence are admissible to show propensity on a pertinent character trait, but specific instances of conduct are not, unless the conduct is an essential element of a claim or defense. *People v. Goldfuss*, 98 P.3d 935 (Colo. App. 2004).

Explanation

The evidence of a person's character is generally inadmissible as irrelevant when offered on the issue of that person's propensity to act in conformity with such character trait. When a criminal defendant puts in issue his or her own character or puts in issue the character of the alleged victim, opinion and reputation evidence is admissible. Sufficient foundation for the opinion/reputation evidence must be laid. *Lombardi v. Graham*, 794 P.2d 610 (Colo. 1990). Specific instances of conduct may be inquired into on cross-examination, where there is a good faith basis. *People v. Pratt*, 759 P.2d 672 (Colo. 1988). In either a civil or criminal case, where the character of a party is an essential element of a claim, charge, or defense, specific instances of conduct and opinion or reputation evidence is admissible under CRE 405(b).

CHARACTER EVIDENCE: ACCUSED OR VICTIM IN A CRIMINAL CASE

Objections

- *I object. The prosecution is attempting to offer evidence of the defendant's character where the defendant has not offered any character evidence.*

- *I object. The prosecution is attempting to offer evidence of the victim's character where none has been offered by the defendant.*

- *I object. The defendant is offering improper character evidence of the victim.*

Responses

- *The defendant has opened the door on his (her) character by offering evidence of his (her) pertinent character trait.*

- *The defendant's character is an essential element of the charge or defense.*

- *The defendant has opened the door to examine the victim's character by:*

  - *» offering evidence of the victim's character,* or

  - *» offering evidence that the victim was the first aggressor in a homicide case.*

- *The defense is entitled to offer character evidence by reputation or opinion evidence of the victim's character for violence, or that a specific incident demonstrating the victim's violent character was known by the defendant before the act here charged, and thus goes to the reasonableness of the defendant's actions.*

Cross-Reference to Colorado Rules 404 and 405

When lay opinion testimony is offered on a pertinent character trait, the opinion must be based on the witness's own personal knowledge. *Lombardi v. Graham*, 794 P.2d 610 (Colo. 1990).

Under CRE 405(b), specific prior acts of violence are not admissible to show the victim was the initial aggressor where the defendant was not aware of prior acts. However, reputation and opinion evidence are admissible. *People v. Jones*, 675 P.2d 9 (Colo. 1984); *People v. Ferguson*, 43 P.3d 705 (Colo. App. 2001).

When an examiner proposes to impeach a character witness's testimony by inquiring into specific instances of conduct under Rule 405(a), the proponent must have a good faith basis to do so and be prepared to demonstrate and obtain a pre-inquiry ruling in camera that acts are relevant and actually occurred. *People v. Pratt*, 759 P.2d 676, 684 (Colo. 1988); *People v. Dembry*, 91 P.3d 431 (Colo. App. 2003).

The defendant may open the door to specific instances of criminal conduct that are not convictions by making broad generalizations about defendant's law-abiding character. *People v. Yaklich*, 744 P.2d

504 (Colo. 1987); *People v. Mershon*, 844 P.2d 1240 (Colo. App. 1992), *aff'd and reversed on other grounds*, *People v. Mershon*, 874 P.2d 1025 (Colo. 1994).

Explanation

Where the accused in a criminal case opens the door to his or her own good character pursuant to Rule 404(a)(1) or to the victim's character pursuant to Rule 404(a)(2), then the prosecution is permitted to rebut that evidence with contrary character evidence. Evidence of the defendant's character for aggressiveness or violence is admissible when the accused offers similar evidence about the victim. Rule 404(a)(1) permits a criminal defendant to offer reputation or opinion evidence, through a character witness, to show lack of propensity to commit the crime charged. Rule 404(a)(2) allows the criminal defendant to offer evidence of the victim's relevant character trait to show the propensity of the victim to act in a certain way where pertinent. Pursuant to Rule 404(a)(1) and Rule 404(a)(2), character evidence may only be proved by reputation or opinion evidence in a criminal case.

Pursuant to Rule 405(b), in both civil and criminal cases, if character is an essential element of the charge, claim, or defense, that character trait may be proved by specific instances of conduct, in addition to, in criminal cases, the admission of reputation and opinion evidence.

CHARACTER EVIDENCE: OTHER ACTS, CRIMES, OR WRONGS

Objection

- *I object. This evidence is inadmissible character evidence offered on propensity.*

Response

- *This evidence is not offered on propensity, but rather for the purpose of showing* (state purpose), *a relevant, non-propensity purpose pursuant to Rule 404(b). Evidence of other crimes, wrongs, or acts is not admissible to prove the character of a person in order to show action in conformity therewith. Such evidence may be admissible, however, for other purposes, such as proof of motive, opportunity, intent, plan, knowledge, identity, or absence of mistake or accident.*

Cross-Reference to Colorado Rule 404(b)

Unlike the procedure approved in *U.S. v. Huddleston*, 485 U.S. 681 (1988), Colorado requires that the admissibility of other transaction evidence be determined in camera and that the defendant's participation be established by a preponderance of the evidence. *People v. Garner*, 806 P.2d 366 (Colo. 1991). Other transaction evidence is admissible, if the proponent establishes a) by a preponderance of the evidence that the party committed the other act; b) the evidence is admissible for a valid purpose and is logically relevant; c) the relevance is independent of the intermediate inference that the actor is of bad character; and d) the probative value is not substantially outweighed by the danger of unfair prejudice. *Yusem v. People*, 210 P.3d 458 (Colo. 2009); *Masters v. People*, 58 P.3d 979 (Colo. 2002). Colorado has approved the use of the doctrine of chances to establish prongs b) and c) above: logical relevance and the dispelling of the intermediate inference of bad character. *People v. Jones*, 2013 CO 59. Colorado has a specific notice requirement under Rule 404(b), when specifically requested by the accused, unless excused for good cause shown. Upon a proper showing, the defense can use 404(b) evidence. *People v. Salazar*, 272 P.3d 1087 (Colo. 2012)

Similar transaction evidence is admissible in civil cases. *Boettcher v. Munson*, 854 P.2d 199 (Colo. 1993). The court must give a limited purpose instruction only upon request. *O'Neal v. Reliance Mtg. Co.*, 721 P.2d 1230 (Colo. App. 1984).

In sexual assault cases, the court must, *sua sponte*, inform the jury of the limited purpose of the other transaction evidence. C.R.S. § 16-10-301. In sexual assault cases, the prosecution must establish a prima facie case before the evidence is admissible and the court must use the same procedure in determining admissibility under CRE 404(b). *Adrian v. People*,

770 P.2d 1243 (Colo. 1989); *Bondsteel v. People*, 439 P.3d 847 (Colo. 2019); *People v. Larson*, 97 P.3d 246 (Colo. App. 2004). Colorado Revised Statute § 18-6-801.5 permits the admission of other acts of domestic violence between the accused and the alleged victim when a) notice of a proper purpose is given by the proponent; b) the court conducts a balancing test under Rule 403; (c) the court gives a limiting instruction when the evidence is received and during final instructions; and (d) the proponent establish by a preponderance of the evidence that the defendant committed the other acts. *People v. Torres*, 141 P.3d 931 (Colo. App. 2006). The fact that the defendant has been acquitted of the other act does not bar its admission and evidence of the acquittal is admissible in the court's discretion. *People v. Kinney*, 187 P.3d 548 (Colo. 2008).

Other act evidence may be received as *res gestae* evidence. That is evidence that is contemporaneous with and serves to illustrate the character of the charged offense. *People v. Rollins*, 892 P.2d 866 (Colo. 1995); *People v. Coney*, 98 P.3d (Colo. App. 2004). No limiting instruction is required for *res gestae* evidence.

Evidence of a defendant's prior alcohol driving offenses is admissible to show willful and wanton conduct, in request for exemplary damages. *Alhilo v. Kliem*, 2016 COA 142.

Explanation

Rule 404(b) is not an exception to the general rule forbidding the use of character evidence to show propensity. Rather, Rule 404(b) admits character evidence where it involves specific crimes, wrongs, or acts, other than those involved in the case at bar, for any relevant, non-propensity purpose, including the commonly enumerated purposes illustrated in the rule.

CHARACTER EVIDENCE: RAPE OR SEX OFFENSE CASES—RELEVANCE OF VICTIM'S PAST BEHAVIOR

Objections

- (opinion or reputation evidence) *I object. The question calls for opinion or reputation evidence concerning the alleged victim's sexual activity.*

- (specific instances of prior sexual activity) *I object. The proffered evidence of prior sexual activity on the part of the alleged victim is irrelevant.*

Responses

- (opinion or reputation evidence) *There is no appropriate response.*

- *The evidence of prior sexual activity was between the complainant and the defendant. Proper notice has been given, and the court has determined the evidence is relevant.*

- *The evidence of prior sexual behavior is offered for the purpose of showing that the act or acts charged were not committed by the defendant. Proper notice has been given, and the court has determined the evidence is relevant.*

- *The evidence of prior sexual activity is evidence of a pattern of sexual behavior so distinctive and so closely resembling the defendant's version as to tend to prove that the complainant consented or that the complainant behaved in such a manner as to lead the defendant to reasonably believe the complainant consented. Proper notice has been given, and the court has determined the evidence is relevant.*

* *The evidence is offered as the basis of expert psychological or psychiatric opinion that the complainant fantasized or invented the acts or acts charged. Proper notice has been given, and the court has determined the evidence is relevant.*

Cross-Reference to Colorado Rule 412

Colorado has no rule counterpart to Federal Rule of Evidence 412. C.R.S. § 18-3-407 and § 13-25-138 govern the admission of a victim's sexual history. The statute makes it a rebuttable presumption that a victim's sexual activity is irrelevant. There are two exceptions: 1) evidence of prior or subsequent sexual conduct with the accused, and 2) evidence of specific acts of sexual contact showing source of semen, disease, or pregnancy offered to show the act charged was not committed by the defendant. *People v. Williamson*, 249 P.3d 801, 802 (Colo. 2011). In these two situations, the defendant need not obtain a pre-inquiry ruling of admissibility. *People v. Martinez*, 634 P.2d 26 (Colo. 1981).

In all other situations, such as where defendant wants to offer evidence of victim's false reporting of sexual assaults or the defendant asserts that the alleged victim's sexual history admissible, the defendant must follow a strict procedure demonstrating relevancy to a material issue in the case and obtain a ruling of admissibility before inquiry is permitted. *People v. Weiss*, 133 P.3d 1180 (Colo. 2006); *In Re People v. Bryant*, 94 P.3d 624 (Colo. 2004); *People v. Marx*, 2019 COA 138.

Character Evidence: Truthful or Untruthful Character

Objections

- *I object. Insufficient character foundation. Opposing counsel is attempting to elicit truthful character testimony when the witness's character for truthfulness has not been attacked.*

- *I object. Counsel is attempting to offer extrinsic evidence of specific incidents of untruthful character.*

- *I object. Counsel is attempting to offer testimony that the witness was truthful on a particular occasion.*

Responses

- *The truthful character of* (name of witness) *was attacked in the following manner* (describe).

- *Extrinsic evidence of a specific instance of untruthful character is admissible when it relates to a felony conviction to impeach the witness under C.R.S. § 13-90-101.*

- *There is no response to an objection that the question seeks to elicit testimony about truthfulness on a particular occasion.*

Cross-Reference to Colorado Rule 608

By testifying, a party does not automatically place their character for truthfulness at issue. *People v. Miller*, 890 P.2d 84 (Colo. 1995).

Explanation

Rule 608(a) permits reputation and opinion evidence for truthful character only when the witness's truthful character is attacked. Pointing out inconsistencies in two stories is an insufficient foundation to elicit truthful character testimony. *People v. Wheatley*, 805 P.2d 1148 (Colo. App. 1990). A witness or party may not comment on another's truthfulness on a particular occasion. *Liggett v. People*, 135 P.3d 725, (Colo. 2006). Nor may an expert testify that children tend not to fabricate sexual contact. *People v. Wittrein*, 221 P.3d 1076 (Colo. 2009).

Under Rule 608(b), specific instances of untruthfulness may be inquired into on cross-examination in the court's discretion. *People v. Distel*, 759 P.2d 654 (Colo. 1988). Untruthfulness has an expansive definition to include any dishonest conduct. *People v. Segovia*, 196 P.3d 1126 (Colo. 2008) (shoplifting); *People v. Campos*, 2015 COA 47 (using false SSN); *Leaf v. Beihoffer*, 2014 COA 117 (failure to file tax return). Extrinsic evidence is not admissible to prove the specific instances of untruthfulness. *People v. Caldwell*, 43 P.3d 663 (Colo. App. 2001). However, where the evidence is being offered as impeachment by contradiction, extrinsic evidence is admissible. *People v. Hall*, 107 P.3d 1073 (Colo. App. 2004).

COMPETENCE TO TESTIFY

Objections

- *I object to the calling of this witness on the ground of incompetence to testify because the witness lacks the ability to* (state relevant reason), *which has been shown on the voir dire of the witness.*

- *I move to strike the witness's testimony and object to further testimony on the ground that the witness is incompetent in that his* (her) *testimony has shown the inability to* (state relevant reason).

Responses

- *The witness is competent because he* (she) *is capable of expressing himself* (herself) *directly or through an interpreter.*

- *The witness is competent because he* (she) *is capable of understanding his* (her) *duty to testify truthfully.*

- *The witness is competent to testify and any questions regarding the witness's testimonial capacity go to the weight of the evidence rather than the competency of the witness.*

Cross-Reference to Colorado Rules 601, 602, 603, 604, 605, and 606

In Colorado, Rule 601 provides that all witnesses are competent except as may be limited by rule or statute. There are no limitations by rule, except the requirement of an oath or affirmation that interpreters qualify as an expert and prohibiting judges as witnesses in cases in which they preside. CRE 603, 604, and 605, respectively.

With the exception of privileges, statutory provisions C.R.S. §§ 13-90-102 through -106 govern the issue of competency.

In Colorado, Rule 606 does not require a party to object to a juror as a witness to preserve the issue for review. Jurors' statements are admissible to impeach a verdict, when related to extrinsic influences, but not confusion or undue pressure. *People v. Harlan*, 109 P.3d 616 (Colo. 2005); *Hall v. Levine*, 104 P.3d 222 (Colo. 2005); *People v. Wadle*, 97 P.3d 932 (Colo. 2004). Extrinsic influences do not prohibit jurors from relying on their professional and educational expertise to inform their deliberations. *People v. Perez*, 367 P.3d 695 (Colo. 2016).

In *Pena-Rodriguez v. Colorado*, 580 U.S. ___, ___, 137 S.Ct. 855, 867 (2017), the Court recognized an exception to Rule 606(b)'s no-impeachment rule "when a juror's statements indicate that racial animus was a significant motivating factor in his or her finding of guilt."

Explanation

The statutory limitations on competency, other than those relating to privilege are 1) the Dead Man's Statute, C.R.S. § 13-90-102; 2) conversations with a deceased partner when offered by a party adverse to the surviving partner, C.R.S. § 13-90-104; 3) persons of unsound mind, C.R.S. § 13-90-105; and 4) children under age ten who cannot receive just impressions of the facts upon which they are examined or cannot relate those facts truly, C.R.S. § 13-90-106(1)(b)(I). The child competency requirement does not apply in civil or criminal child abuse or sexual assault cases, when the child can describe the events in age-appropriate language. C.R.S. § 13-90-106(1)(b)(II). The competency hearing for the child must be held outside the presence of the jury, when so requested by the defendant. *People v. Wittrein*, 221 P.3d 1076 (Colo. 2009).

A witness who is compensated based on a percentage of the damages awarded, is not *per se* incompetent to testify. *Murray v. Just in Case Lighthouse, LLC*, 374 P.3d 443 (Colo. 2016).

COMPOUND QUESTIONS

Objection

• *I object. The question is compound.*

Response

• *I withdraw the question and will rephrase.*

Cross-Reference to Colorado Rule 611(a)

Rule 611(a) allows the court to control the mode and order of presenting the evidence.

Explanation

A compound question asks for two or more items of information at the same time. Thus, it is impossible to understand the answer's meaning. Objections to compound questions should be made when the answer is likely to mislead the jury to the detriment of objecting counsel's client. Otherwise, the objection merely makes the opponent a better questioner.

COMPROMISE/OFFERS OF COMPROMISE

Objection

• *I object. The proffered evidence is evidence of compromise negotiations offered on liability and/or damages.*

Responses

• *The evidence is admissible because:*
  » *there was no dispute between the parties at the time of the compromise discussions,* or
  » *the evidence is not offered on liability or damage issues but rather, for another purpose, such as to show bias, no undue delay, or an effort to subvert a criminal investigation.*

Cross-Reference to Colorado Rule 408

In addition to CRE 408, Colorado has a statute, C.R.S. § 13-22-307, that prohibits disclosure of statements made during mediation or dispute resolution sessions. *Yaekle v. Andrews*, 195 P.3d 1101 (Colo. 2008).

CRE only applies to civil cases, not criminal cases. *People v. Butson*, 410 P.3d 744 (Colo. App. 2017).

Explanation

Evidence of settlement or of settlement negotiations in a disputed civil claim is inadmissible to prove

---

liability or the amount of the claim. Evidence of settlement, offers to settle, or statements made during the course of settlement negotiations may be admissible for another relevant purpose, e.g., to show bias, to negate allegations of undue delay, or as an effort to subvert a criminal investigation or prosecution. *Hartman v. Community Responsibility Ctr.*, 87 P.3d 202 (Colo. App. 2003); *Guarantee v. King*, 97 P.3d 161 (Colo. App. 2003) (admission of statements in mediation to show knowledge under CRE 408—opponent waived objection under mediator communication confidentiality statute).

CROSS-EXAMINATION: GENERALLY

Objection

• *I move to strike the direct testimony of the witness because I have not had the opportunity to conduct a full and fair cross-examination. I ask that the jury be instructed to disregard the testimony of the witness.*

Responses

• *The purposes of cross-examination have been substantially completed.*

• *Counsel has waived the right to a full and complete cross-examination by* (insert reasons).

Cross-Reference to Colorado Rule

There is no Colorado Rule which specifically addresses the issue of the right to a full and fair cross-examination. However, where cross-examination is so limited as to be a denial of right to cross-examine, the restriction is a due process violation and in a criminal case a right to full confrontation. *People v. Dunham,* 2016 COA 73; *People v. Bowman,* 669 P.2d 1369 (Colo. 1983); *People v. McKinney,* 80 P.3d 823 (Colo. App. 2003).

Explanation

As to every witness presented by a party, the adverse party has the right to a full and fair cross-examination.

The remedy for the denial of such right is to have the testimony stricken from the record or to have a new trial granted.

CROSS-EXAMINATION: SCOPE

Objection

• *I object. The question on cross-examination exceeds the proper scope of cross-examination.*

Responses

• *The subject matter of the question is relevant to a specific issue in the case.*

• *The question seeks to elicit information that is relevant to the credibility of the witness.*

Cross-Reference to Colorado Rule

There is no Colorado Rule that specifically addresses the issue of the right to a full and fair cross-examination. Cross-examination should be limited to the subject matter of the direct examination and matters affecting the credibility of the witness. CRE 611(b). However, where cross-examination is so limited as to be a denial of the right to cross-examine, especially on credibility issues, the restriction is a due process/confrontation clause violation. *People v. Dunham*, 2016 COA 73; *People v. Bowman*, 669 P.2d 1369 (Colo. 1983); *People v. McKinney*, 80 P.3d 823 (Colo. App. 2003). Re-cross-examination may be limited when of marginal utility or when the redirect only covered the content of direct. *People v. Kerber*, 64 P.3d 930 (Colo. App. 2002).

Explanation

As to every witness presented by a party, the adverse party has the right to a full and fair cross-examination. The remedy for the denial of such right is to have the testimony stricken from the record.

DEAD MAN'S STATUTE

Objections

- *I object. The witness's testimony violates the Dead Man's Statute.*
- *I object. The witness is incompetent to testify.*

Responses

- *The witness's testimony does not concern an oral communication between the decedent and himself* (herself).

- *The witness is not a party with a direct interest in the outcome of the litigation* (or the witness is not a person from whom the interest is derived).

- *The statement was made under oath, when the person was competent to testify.*

- *The statement is corroborated by independent material evidence, which is trustworthy.*

- *The opposing party has already elicited un-corroborated evidence of related communications.*

- *The party's testimony is against his* (her) *own interest.*

Cross-Reference to Colorado Rule

The Colorado version of the Dead Man's Statute is codified at C.R.S. § 13-90-102. The legislature dramatically liberalized the Dead Man's Statute. *In re Estate of Crenshaw*, 100 P.3d 568 (Colo. App. 2004); *Glover v. Innis*, 252 P.3d 1204, 1207 (Colo. App. 2011).

Explanation

The Dead Man's Statute prohibits an interested witness from testifying to a conversation with a deceased person or mentally incompetent person. The statute limits the admissibility of statements made by persons who are incapable of testifying, and "guard(s) against perjury by living interested witnesses, when deceased/incompetent person cannot refute the testimony, thus protecting estates against unjust claims." *In re Estate of Crenshaw*, 100 P.3d 568, 569 (Colo. App. 2004).

EXHIBITS: DEMONSTRATIVE

Objections

- *I object. The proffered exhibit has not been properly authenticated.*

- (to-scale model) *I object. The proffered exhibit has not been shown to be a fair and accurate representation of an object or thing in issue in this case.*

Responses

- *The demonstrative exhibit has been authenticated by the testimony of* (insert name of witness). *The witness has testified that:*

  » (to-scale models) *the exhibit is a fair and accurate representation of a scene in issue,* or

  » *the witness has testified that the exhibit is a to-scale model and is a fair and accurate representation of an object that is in issue.*

Cross-Reference to Colorado Rule

There is no specific rule on demonstrative exhibits. All exhibits must be authenticated pursuant to Rule 901(a).

Explanation

Typical demonstrative exhibits are to-scale models and sufficiently identical duplicates of the actual real evidence. The requirement of authentication of such exhibits is satisfied by evidence sufficient to support a finding that the exhibit is a fair and accurate depiction or representation of something that is in issue in a case. *People v. Brown*, 313 P.3d 608, footnote 3, (Colo. App. 2011).

Demonstrative aids can take various forms, including diagrams, maps, computer animations, or, as relevant here, models or mock-ups and their use should be encouraged because they give the jurors and the court a clear comprehension of the physical facts, certainly much clearer than one would be able to describe in words. *People v. Palacios*, 419 P.3d 1014 (Colo. App. 2018).

EXHIBITS: ILLUSTRATIVE

Objections

- *I object. The proffered illustrative exhibit has not been properly authenticated.*
- *I object. The proffered exhibit has not been shown to be a fair and accurate depiction of a relevant scene.*
- *I object. The proffered illustrative exhibit is confusing and/or misleading.*
- *I object. The proffered illustrative exhibit contains markings that will lead the witness in reciting testimony.*

Responses

- (photographs) *The witness has testified that the photograph shows a relevant scene as it appeared at a relevant time, the exhibit is a fair and accurate depiction of that scene, and the exhibit will aid in illustrating the witness's testimony.*

- *The illustrative exhibit has been authenticated by the testimony of* (insert name of witness). *The witness testified that:*

  » *the witness recognizes what the exhibit portrays, and that the exhibit will aid in illustrating and* (or) *explaining the witness's testimony.*

  » *the exhibit is not offered as a to-scale diagram; it is merely an aid to the explaining of testimony. Any matters affecting the weight to be given the*

D
E
F

illustrative exhibit can be demonstrated during cross-examination.

» (insert name of witness) *has already testified as to what the markings contained on the exhibit portray. The exhibit is offered merely to illustrate that testimony.*

Cross-Reference to Colorado Rule

There is no specific rule on illustrative exhibits. All exhibits must be authenticated pursuant to Rule 901(a).

Explanation

Illustrative exhibits are those which assist a witness in testifying. Examples of illustrative exhibits are diagrams, charts, graphs, and photographs (although photographs may also be introduced as substantive evidence). The requirement of authentication is satisfied as to illustrative exhibits by testimony that the exhibit will aid the witness to illustrate or explain his or her testimony. *People v. Brown*, 313 P.3d 608, footnote 3 (Colo. App. 2011) (comparing demonstrative, illustrative, real or physical evidence).

Exhibits: Tangible Objects

Objection

- *I object. The proffered exhibit is incompetent for lack of proper foundation.*

Response

- *I have shown through the testimony of* (insert name of witness) *that he* (she) *perceived the exhibit at a relevant time, the exhibit is the one perceived, and it is in substantially the same condition as it was at the relevant time.*

Cross-Reference to Colorado Rule

There is no specific rule on tangible objects exhibits. All exhibits must be authenticated pursuant to Rule 901(a). Once the proponent has established that the item is what it is claimed to be, imperfections in the chain of custody go to the weight to be accorded to the evidence, not the admissibility. *People v. Grace,* 55 P.3d 165 (Colo. App. 2001).

Explanation

In order to admit a tangible object, also referred to as "real" evidence, the proponent must show that it can be identified by a witness who had knowledge of the tangible object at a relevant time and who can testify that the tangible object is in the same or substantially the same condition as it was at a relevant time. *People v. Brown,* 313 P.3d 608 (Colo. App. 2011).

EXHIBITS: WRITINGS

Objections

- *I object to the introduction of this exhibit. There is an improper foundation because:*
  - » *it is not relevant,* or
  - » *has not been authenticated,* or
  - » *has not met the original document rule,* or
  - » *the writing is hearsay.*

Response

- *The foundational requirements regarding relevance, authentication, the original document rule, and hearsay have been met through the testimony of* (insert names of witnesses) *who have testified that* (insert a portion of the relevant testimony).

Cross-Reference to Colorado Rule

Relevance is governed by rules in Article 4, authenticity is governed by rules in Article 9, original documents rule concerns are governed by rules in Article 10, and hearsay is governed by rules in Article 8.

Explanation

In order to introduce a writing in evidence, the proponent must meet four foundational requirements. The writing must be shown to be relevant, to be authentic, to meet the requirements of the original document rule, and either to qualify as non-hearsay or to meet an exception to the hearsay rule. The probative value of the exhibit cannot be substantially outweighed by unfair prejudice. Rule 403.

D
E
F

EXPERT OPINION

Objections

- *I object to the qualification of the witness as an expert.*
- *I object to the admission of expert testimony because the discipline in which the witness purports to qualify as an expert is not considered to be sufficiently reliable in the field to which it belongs.*
- *I object to the admission of the witness's opinion because it is beyond the area of expertise in which he* (she) *has been qualified.*

Responses

- *I have shown that the witness is qualified as an expert in* (insert field of expertise) *through the witness's knowledge, skill, experience, training, or education.*
- *I have shown that the area of expertise in which the witness is qualified or the witness's methodology is considered sufficiently reliable in the branch of the discipline to which it belongs. The court has qualified the expert in the area of* (insert field of expertise) *and the witness's opinion is within that area.*

Cross-Reference to Colorado Rules 702, 703, 704, 705, and 706

The test for expert qualification is whether this witness can be of assistance to the jury on this issue. *Masters v. People*, 58 P.3d 979 (Colo. 2002). In medical malpractice cases, an expert can opine on the issue of standard of care in a specialty other than the expert's own specialty when there is a showing of substantial familiarity and the two specialties are similar. C.R.S. § 13-64-401; *People in Interest of R.D.*, 2012 COA 35. In Colorado, the admissibility of expert opinion testimony is contingent on establishing reliability and relevancy. For the reliability prong, the court may be guided by the factors in *Daubert v. Merrell Dow Pharmaceuticals*, 509 U.S. 579 (1993), and other cases such as *U.S. v. Downing*, 753 F.2d 1224 (3d Cir. 1985). Additionally, satisfaction of the reliability prong is determined by the witness's qualifications to testify on the proffered subject. In determining relevancy, the court will consider the degree to which the evidence will be of assistance to the jury and whether the probative value of the evidence is outweighed by the danger of unfair prejudice. *People v. Shreck*, 22 P.3d 68 (Colo. 2001); *People v. Martinez*, 74 P.3d 316 (Colo. 2003); *People v. Rector*, 248 P.3d 1196 (Colo. 2011) (hearing unnecessary provided sufficient information to make specific findings about the reliability of the scientific principles involved, experts qualifications, helpfulness and prejudice); *People v. Cooper*, 2019 COA 21 (expert testimony must fit the issues in the case). Rule 702 governs the admissibility of novel scientific principles or experience based on specialized knowledge. *Brooks v. People*, 975 P.2d 1105 (Colo. 1999); *Meier v. McCoy*, 119 P.3d 519

(Colo. App. 2004). It is not necessary that the opinion be expressed as a reasonable degree of probability if the expert opinion is otherwise relevant and reliable. *People v. Ramirez*, 155 P.3d 371 (Colo. 2007).

The determination of whether the proffered testimony is lay or expert testimony, the court must look to the basis for the opinion. *Venalonzo v. People*, 2017 CO 9, ¶ 23. Where the witness provides testimony that could be expected to be based on an ordinary person's experiences or knowledge, then the witness is offering lay testimony. *Id.* However, if the witness provides testimony that could not be offered without specialized experiences, knowledge, or training, then the witness is offering expert testimony. *Id.*; *Vigil v. People*, 2019 CO 105 (shoe print evidence-lay opinion); *Campbell v. People*, 443 P.3d 72 (Colo. 2019) (results of Horizontal Gaze Nystagmus test is expert testimony); *People v. Ramos*, 2017 CO 6 (differentiating blood cast-off from blood transfer was expert testimony); *People v. Kubuugu*, 2019 CO 9 (opinion was expert that defendant exuded a metabolized alcohol odor that indicated that he had consumed alcohol prior to entering the apartment complex); *Romero v. People*, 393 P.3d 973 (Colo. 2017) (grooming behavior requires expert opinion testimony); *People v. Garrison*, 411 P.3d 270 (Colo. App. 2017) (collecting cases on whether particular police testimony is lay or expert).

While an expert cannot usurp the jury's function, testimony is admissible under CRE 704 that goes to the ultimate issue in the case. In determining whether the witness testimony usurped the jury's function, the court will analyze whether (1) the witness opined that the defendant committed or likely committed the crime; (2) the testimony was clarified on cross-examination; (3) the expert's testimony usurped the trial court's function by expressing an opinion on the applicable law or legal standard; and (4) the jury was properly instructed on the law and that it could accept or reject the witness's opinion. *People v. Rector*, 248 P.3d 1196, 1203 (Colo. 2011); *People v. Payne*, 2019 COA 167. Rule 704 does not allow a witness to testify about whether a particular legal standard has been met. *Taylor Morrison of Colo., Inc v. Terracon Consultants, Inc.*, 410 P.3d 767 (Colo. App. 2017).

Under CRE 706(a), the court may appoint any expert witnesses agreed upon by the parties and may appoint expert witnesses of its own selection. *Cielo Vista Ranch I, LLC v. Alire*, 433 P.3d 596 (Colo. App. 2018).

Explanation

Where the proponent seeks to offer opinions, conclusions, or inferences to assist the fact-finder in determining a fact in issue and such opinions are beyond the ability of the fact-finder, the proponent may offer such opinions, conclusions, or inferences from a witness

FIRSTHAND KNOWLEDGE

Objection

• *I object. There has been no foundation to show the witness has personal knowledge of the matter about which he or she has been asked.*

Response

• *The witness has shown firsthand knowledge of the subject matter of the witness's testimony. A foundation has been laid which demonstrates the witness was in a position to know those items about which his or her testimony will be given.*

Cross-Reference to Colorado Rule 602

The threshold for establishing personal knowledge is not very high and may be established circumstantially. *People v. Garcia*, 826 P.2d 1259 (Colo. 2001). The rule of personal knowledge does not apply to expert witnesses. *People v. Valencia*, 257 P.3d 1203, 1208 (Colo. App. 2011). Personal knowledge for summary witness satisfied by personal review of underlying documents. *Murray v. Just in Case Lighthouse, LLC*, 374 P.3d 443 (Colo. 2016). Statements by a party-opponent need not be based on personal knowledge. *People v. Sparks*, 434 P.3d 713 (Colo. App. 2018).

Explanation

A witness may testify only as to the matters about which he or she has personal or firsthand knowledge. Lack of personal knowledge makes the witness incompetent to testify as to particular facts. Generally, the proponent of the witness must lay a foundation on the issue of personal knowledge by offering evidence sufficient to support a finding that the witness has firsthand knowledge of the subject matter about which testimony will be given.

GUILTY PLEAS (OFFERS OF PLEAS AND RELATED STATEMENTS)

Objection

- *I object that this evidence is inadmissible as a withdrawn guilty plea, no contest plea, or as an offer to so plead.*

Responses

- *This evidence is admissible against the criminal defendant because the statement is being offered for impeachment purposes and the statement is voluntary and reliable and made on the record.*

- *The evidence is admissible in this perjury prosecution because the statement was made on the record and the statement is voluntary and reliable.*

Cross-Reference to Colorado Rule 410

Generally, withdrawn guilty or *nolo contendere* pleas and statements made during those pleas are not admissible. Colorado takes a broad interpretation of the phrase "statements made in any connection with" plea bargains. *People v. Garcia*, 169 P.3d 223, 228 (Colo. App. 2007). Withdrawn guilty or *nolo contendere* pleas can be used for impeachment purposes and perjury prosecutions, as long as the pleas are voluntary, of record, and reliable.

Explanation

Colorado has no provision for allowing withdrawn pleas to be used to put other plea statements in context. Colorado does not require the statement be under oath or that counsel be present. Statements of willingness to plead guilty to the police that the prosecutor is unaware of are not subject to the CRE 410 bar. *People v. Martinez*, 36 P.3d 154 (Colo. App. 2001).

HABIT AND ROUTINE PRACTICE

Objection

- *I object. This evidence is irrelevant as a prior act offered on the issue of propensity.*

Response

- *This evidence is relevant because it shows a consistent habit or routine practice that raises a permissible inference that the party or organization likely acted in this case according to the habit or routine practice.*

Cross-Reference to Colorado Rule 406 Explanation

Evidence of a personal habit or of the routine practice of an organization is admissible as relevant to how that on a specific occasion, such person or organization acted in conformity with the proffered habit or practice. By its nature, habit or routine practice testimony is circumstantial proof that certain conduct, or an act consistent therewith, occurred. *People in the Interest of T.R.*, 860 P.2d 559 (Colo. App. 1993). Habit or routine practice evidence is admissible even when there is firsthand evidence of the conduct in question.

Hearsay: Generally

Objections
- *I object. The question calls for a hearsay answer.*
- *I move to strike the answer as hearsay.*

Responses
- *The statement is not being offered for the truth of the matter asserted. Instead, it is offered to show the statement was made. The making of the statement in question is relevant to show:*
    - » *the effect on a person who heard the statement,* or
    - » *a prior inconsistent statement,* or
    - » *an operative legal fact or a verbal act,* or
    - » *the knowledge of the declarant,* or
    - » *corroboration of the testifying witness.*

Cross-Reference to Colorado Rule 801

Colorado's definition of statement includes oral or written assertion and conduct that is intended to be communicative. If the statement is offered to show the effect on the hearer, it is not hearsay. *People v. Todd*, 538 P.2d 433 (Colo. 1973); *People v. Banks*, 983 P.2d 102 (Colo. App. 1999). When the statements are offered to put into context other non-hearsay statements, then the proffered statements are not hearsay. *Mclaughlin v. BNSF*, 2012 COA 92; *People v. Arnold*, 826 P.2d 365 (Colo. App. 1991). If offered as notice to hearer, the statements are not hearsay. *Schumtz v. Bolles,* 800 P.2d 1307 (Colo. 1990); *Vista Resorts v. Goodyear,* 117 P.3d 60 (Colo. App. 2005). If the statements are offered to prove their falsity, they are not hearsay. *People v. Godinez,* 2018 COA 170. Finally, where the words have independent legal significance they are not hearsay. *Conrad v. City and County of Denver,* 656 P.2d 662 (Colo. 1982); *People v. Dominguez,* 2019 COA 78 (texts of drug purchase inquiry as verbal act). A translation may or may not be hearsay depending upon the factual circumstances. *People v. Hinojos-Mendoza,* 140 P.3d 30 (Colo. App. 2006), *rev'd on other grounds,* 169 P.3d 662 (2007). A properly authenticated, machine-generated report is not hearsay, but a person recounting what the report says is hearsay. *People v. Hamilton,* 2019 COA 101.

Explanation

The foolproof hearsay test: Ask the question whether the relevant purpose for offering the out-of-court statement is its truth. If the answer to that question is *yes,* the out-of-court statement is hearsay. If the answer to the question is not clearly *yes,* ask this next question: "Must the content of the out-of-court statement be believed in order to be relevant?" If the answer to this follow-up question is *yes,* the evidence is hearsay. *People v. Kendall,* 174 P.3d 791 (Colo. App. 2007). However, evidence of a prior consistent statement of a testifying witness is not hearsay when it is offered to rehabilitate credibility. *People v. Eppens,* 979 P.2d 14 (Colo. 1999).

Hearsay: Attacking and Supporting the Credibility of a Hearsay Declarant

Objection

G
H

• *I object. The question seeks to attack the credibility of a person who has not appeared as a witness.*

Response

• *The person whose credibility is being attacked is a hearsay declarant, whose statement was offered through the testimony of* (insert name of witness). *This impeachment of an out-of-court declarant is permissible to the same extent available for a testifying witness.*

Cross-Reference to Colorado Rule 806

The impeachment of a hearsay declarant pursuant to Rule 806 includes the use of felony convictions through C.R.S. § 13-90-101. *People v. Dore*, 997 P.2d 1214 (Colo. App. 1999); *People v. Short*, 425 P.3d 1208 (Colo. App. 2018) (under CRE 103, when the defendant offers the remainder of his statement to avoid the prosecution's efforts to mislead the jury by only offering part, the defendant's statement is not subject to impeachment by felony conviction under Rule 806).

Explanation

Impeachment of an out-of-court declarant is permissible to the same extent available for a testifying witness. Impeachment by prior inconsistent statement of a hearsay declarant is permitted despite the inability to confront the declarant with the inconsistency. Impeachment of the hearsay declarant as to bias, interest, prejudice, or improper motive may be accomplished without the usual foundational requirement of denial of the same.

G
H

HEARSAY WITHIN HEARSAY

Objections

- *I object to this statement because it contains inadmissible hearsay within hearsay.*

- *I move to strike the answer because it contains hearsay within hearsay.*

Response

- *Both statements are admissible because each either comes within a hearsay exception or is non-hearsay.*

Cross-Reference to Colorado Rule 805 Explanation

To admit hearsay within hearsay, the proponent must account for both out-of-court statements with either a hearsay exception or an argument that the out-of-court statement is offered for a relevant, non-hearsay purpose. *People v. Guilbeaux*, 761 P.2d 255 (Colo. 1988); *People v. Phillips*, 315 P.3d 136 (Colo. App. 2012); *Leiting v. Mutha*, 58 P.3d 1049 (Colo. App. 2002).

Hearsay: Non-Hearsay Admissions

Objections

- *I object. The question calls for a hearsay answer.*
- *I move to strike the answer as hearsay.*

Responses

- *The statement is not hearsay pursuant to Rule 801(d) because I have shown that:*

  - » *the testimony is a prior inconsistent statement under 801(d)(1)(A), or*

  - » *the testimony is a prior consistent statement under 801(d)(1)(B) to rebut a charge of improper motive, recent fabrication, or undue inference, or*

  - » *the statement is one of identification after the witness saw the person under 801(d)(1)(C), or*

  - » *the statement was made by the party opponent under 801(d)(2)(A), or*

  - » *the statement was made by a person and was adopted by the party opponent as the party's own and thus is a vicarious admission of the party opponent under 801(d)(2)(B), or*

  - » *the statement was made by an agent authorized to speak on behalf of a party opponent and thus is a vicarious admission of the party opponent under 801(d)(2)(C), or*

> » *the statement was made by an agent or servant of the party opponent concerning a matter within the scope of the declarant's agency or employment, and was made during the existence of the declarant's agency or employment, and thus is a vicarious admission of a party opponent under 801(d)(2)(D), or*

> » *the statement was made by a co-conspirator of the party opponent during the course of the conspiracy and in furtherance of the conspiracy, and thus is a vicarious admission of the party opponent under 801(d)(2)(E).*

Cross-Reference to Colorado Rule 801(d)

By rule variation and/or case decision, there are several significant differences between the Colorado and Federal Rule 801(d).

Prior inconsistent statements do not have to be under oath to be admissible. In a criminal case, admissibility of prior inconsistent statements is initially determined by C.R.S. § 16-10-201. *Montoya v. People*, 740 P.2d 992 (Colo. 1987); *People v. Candelaria*, 107 P.3d 1080 (Colo. App. 2005), *rev'd on other grounds*, 148 P.3d 178 (Colo. 2006). In civil cases the foundational requirement for admissibility of prior inconsistent statements is determined by whether the statement is being offered for impeachment or substantive purposes —if impeachment, Rule 613 governs; if substantive,

Rule 801(d)(1)(A) governs. The prior statement must be of material variance from trial testimony. *Lisco v. Pinson*, 93 P.3d 1149 (Colo. App. 2003).

Prior consistent statements are admissible to refute claims of recent fabrication, improper motive, and undue influence if the prior consistent statement is made prior to the time the reason to fabricate or improper motive arose. *Tome v. U.S.*, 115 S.Ct. 696 (1995). If the prior consistent statement is being offered to generally rehabilitate the witness, the prior consistent statement can be made at any time. *People v. Eppens*, 979 P.2d 14 (Colo. 1999); *Mclaughlin v. BNSF*, 2012 COA 92; *People v. Elie*, 148 P.3d 359 (Colo. App. 2006).

When offering a statement as an adoptive admission by silence, the proponent must establish that the circumstances demonstrate that the party acquiesced in a statement, thus manifesting a belief in the truth of the statement. *Mullins v. Medical Lien Management*, 2013 COA 134; *People v. Sweeney*, 78 P.3d 1133 (Colo. App. 2003); *People v. Green*, 629 P.2d 1098 (Colo. App. 1981).

Statements of an agent are admissible, if there exists circumstantial evidence of an agency relationship and the statement is made within the scope of, and during the existence of, the agency relationship. No authorization is required. *South Park v. Northwestern*, 847 P.2d 218 (Colo. App. 1992).

Co-conspirator statement admissibility is determined at trial by the court. The proponent must establish that the conspiracy existed, that the declarant and defendant were members of the conspiracy, and that the statement was made in course and furtherance of the conspiracy. The statement can be used to establish foundation but cannot be the only evidence of the conspiracy. *People v. Montoya,* 753 P.2d 729 (Colo. 1988); *People v. Rivera,* 56 P.3d 1155 (Colo. App. 2002).

Explanation

CRE 801(d) provides that certain statements are not hearsay by definition. These include prior statements that are consistent, inconsistent to current testimony, and statements of identification. Also included are statements of a party opponent that are made in a personal, representative, or imputed capacity.

HEARSAY EXCEPTION: ABSENCE OF ENTRY IN BUSINESS RECORDS

Objections

- *I object. The question calls for a hearsay answer.*
- *I move to strike the answer as hearsay.*

Responses

- *The absence of an entry in this record is admissible to show the non-occurrence of an event pursuant to Rule 803(7). I have shown through the testimony of* (insert name of witness) *who is the custodian of the business records, or other qualified person:*

  » *that a business record exists, pursuant to Rule 803(6),* and

  » *the matter that is not recorded in the record is of a kind for which a record would regularly be made and preserved,* and

  » *the source of the information or other circumstances fail to indicate a lack of trustworthiness.*

Cross-Reference to Colorado Rule 803(6), (7)

Explanation

If the proponent is able to lay a foundation for a record of regularly conducted activity pursuant to

---

Rule 803(6), testimony or the offer of the record for the purpose of demonstrating that a particular entry does not appear in the record is permitted for the purpose of proving that the event, about which the record would have been made, did not occur. *Columbia Sav. v. Zelinger*, 794 P.2d 231, 235 (Colo. 1990).

G
H

HEARSAY EXCEPTION: ABSENCE OF PUBLIC RECORDS OR ENTRY

Objections

- *I object. The question calls for a hearsay answer.*
- *I move to strike the answer as hearsay.*

G
H

Responses

- *The absence of a public record concerning the event in question is admissible to prove that the event did not occur pursuant to Rule 803(10). I have shown that:*
  - » *a public agency or office regularly makes and preserves records of a particular kind of matter,* and
  - » *the document is self-certifying pursuant to Rule 902,* and
  - » *a diligent but unavailing search of such records failed to disclose a record, report, statement, date compilation, or entry, all which tends to show that no such entry exists and no such event took place.*

Cross-Reference to Colorado Rule 803(10)

Explanation

The absence of a public record or entry concerning an event that would normally be the subject of a public record is admissible to prove that the event did not occur. In a criminal case, the prosecutor must give fourteen days' notice, prior to trial of intent to use certified proof of non-existence.

HEARSAY EXCEPTION: EXCITED UTTERANCE

Objections

- *I object. The question calls for a hearsay answer.*
- *I move to strike the answer as hearsay.*

Responses

- *The statement is admissible as an excited utterance pursuant to Rule 803(2).*
- *I have shown through the testimony of* (insert name of witness) *that the statement relates to a startling event or condition and was made while the declarant was under the stress or excitement caused by the event or condition.*

Cross-Reference to Colorado Rule 803(2)

The statement must relate to the event and declarant must still be under the stress or excitement of the event and have personal knowledge of the event. *People v. Garcia*, 826 P.2d 1259 (Colo. 1992); *People v. Garrison*, 109 P.3d 1009 (Colo. App. 2005). The time between event and declaration can be minutes or days. *In re O.E.P.*, 654 P.2d 312 (Colo. 1982). In criminal cases, the court should perform an analysis to ensure statement meets Sixth Confrontation Clause requirements. *Compan v. People*, 121 P.3d 876 (Colo.

2005). A hearsay statement is admissible as an excited utterance if its proponent shows 1) the occurrence or event was sufficiently startling to render inoperative the normal reflective thought processes of an observer; 2) the declarant's statement was a spontaneous reaction to the event; and 3) direct or circumstantial evidence supports an inference that the declarant had the opportunity to observe the startling event. *People v. Hagos*, 250 P.3d 596 (Colo. App. 2009). Colorado has used a multi-factorial approach to determine whether the statement was spontaneous. *Canape v. Peterson*, 878 P.2d 83 (Colo. App. 1994).

Explanation

When the declarant is sufficiently startled into making a spontaneous utterance, the assumption is there was neither sufficient time nor presence of mind to fabricate. The event that gives rise to the statement relating to it must be sufficiently startling, and the statement must be made under the stress of that event, so as to remove the likelihood of self-serving reflection in the making of the statement.

Hearsay Exception: Family Records

Objections

- *I object. The question calls for a hearsay answer.*
- *I move to strike the answer as hearsay.*

Responses

- *This statement is admissible as a family record, pursuant to Rule 803(13).*
- *I have shown through the testimony of* (insert name of witness) *that this is a statement of fact concerning personal or family history, contained in a family Bible, genealogy, or the like.*

Cross-Reference to Colorado Rule 803(13)

Explanation

Statements of personal or family history contained in volumes or in other places where if they were inaccurate would have been corrected are admissible to prove the content of those statements. Note the absence of a requirement of contemporaneity of entry. However, such writing, like any other, must be authenticated. In criminal cases, admission of Rule 803(13) records does not implicate the confrontation clause, because such records are non-testimonial and the individual can be cross-examined. *People v. Hinojos-Mendoza,* 140 P.3d 30 (Colo. App. 2006), *rev'd on other grounds,* 169 P.3d 662 (2007).

HEARSAY EXCEPTION:
FORFEITURE BY WRONGDOING

Cross-Reference to Colorado Rule

Colorado has not adopted the federal Forfeiture by Wrongdoing provision. However, Colorado has recognized a common law exception that is the equivalent of forfeiture by wrongdoing exception. *See People v. Moreno*, 160 P.3d 242 (Colo. 2007).

Explanation

Under Colorado's judicial exception, the proponent must prove, by a preponderance of the evidence, at an in camera hearing 1) a witness is unavailable; 2) the defendant was involved in, or responsible for, procuring the unavailability of the witness; and 3) the defendant acted with the intent to deprive the criminal justice system of evidence. If established, the defendant then forfeits the right to confront the witness in all proceedings in which the witness's statements are otherwise admissible. *Vasquez v. People*, 173 P.3d 1099 (Colo. 2007); *People v. Jackson*, 2018 COA 79.

Hearsay Exception:
Former Testimony

Objections

- *I object. The question calls for a hearsay answer.*
- *I move to strike the answer as hearsay.*

Responses

- *The statement is admissible as former testimony pursuant to Rule 804(b)(1).*
- *I have shown through the testimony of* (insert name of witness) *that:*
  - » *the declarant is unavailable pursuant to Rule 804(a), and the statement is testimony given at another hearing of the same or different proceeding, or in a deposition in the course of the same or different proceeding,* and
  - » *the party against whom it is offered had an opportunity and similar motive to develop the testimony by direct, cross, or redirect examination.*

Cross-Reference to Colorado Rule 804

Preliminary hearing and grand jury testimony do not meet the rule requirement because the examiner lacks the same opportunity and motive to inquire. *People v. Smith*, 597 P.2d 204 (Colo. 1979); *People v. Clark*, 370 P.3d 197 (Colo. App. 2015). In a criminal case, the admission of prior testimony implicates the Sixth Amendment Confrontation Clause. *Crawford v. Washington*, 541 U.S. 36 (2004); *Davis v. Washington*, 547 U.S. 814 (2006); *People v. Fry*, 92 P.3d 970 (Colo. 2004).

Explanation

Former testimony is any testimony given under oath in an earlier proceeding. It is admissible at a later hearing if the declarant is unavailable, and the party against whom it is now offered had the opportunity and a similar motive to develop, by questioning of the declarant, the earlier testimony when it was given. The reliability of these statements is gained from the fact that they were given under oath and could be tested by examination by the party against whom they are now offered.

Hearsay Exception: Judgment as to Personal, Family, or General History, or Boundaries

Objections

- *I object. The question calls for a hearsay answer.*
- *I move to strike the answer as hearsay.*

Response

- *This statement is admissible as a judgment relating to personal, family, or general history, or boundaries pursuant to Rule 803(23). I have shown through the testimony of* (insert name of witness) *that this statement is a judgment offered as proof of matters of personal, family, or general history, or boundaries essential to the judgment, and which are provable by evidence of reputation.*

Cross-Reference to Colorado Rule 803(23)

Explanation

Note: This section must be read in conjunction with Rule 803(19) and 803(20). Rule 803(23) only permits admissibility of such evidence where the judgment proves facts that would be provable by reputation evidence.

HEARSAY EXCEPTION: LEARNED TREATISES

Objections

- *I object. The question calls for a hearsay answer.*
- *I move to strike the answer as hearsay.*

Responses

- *This statement is admissible as a statement contained in a learned treatise pursuant to Rule 803(18). I have shown through the testimony of* (insert name of witness) *that the expert witness has relied on the statement and that it is authoritative.*

- (if on cross-examination) *I have called the statement to the attention of the expert and the statement is contained in a published treatise, periodical, or pamphlet on a subject of history, medicine, or other science or art, which has been established as a reliable authority by the testimony or admission of the expert witness, by other expert testimony, or by judicial notice.*

Cross-Reference to Colorado Rule 803(18)

Colorado's learned treatise hearsay exception allows the court to admit the treatise in addition to having the document read to the jury, if the prerequisite foundation has been established. Colorado has ruled that driver's handbooks are not learned treatises. *Garcia v. Mekonnen*, 156 P.3d 1171, 1173 (Colo. App. 2006).

Explanation

A learned treatise is a book or article established as a reliable authority on a matter, ordinarily the subject of expert opinion, which is called to the attention of an expert witness on cross-examination, or which is relied upon by the expert in direct examination. A foundation for the learned treatise may be laid through the expert who is on the stand, through some other expert, or through the taking of judicial notice by the trial judge of the learned nature of the writing. The learned treatise is admissible to either support or attack the testimony of an expert witness. Note that the treatise may only be read to the jury and may be received as an exhibit in the discretion of the court.

G
H

HEARSAY EXCEPTION: MARKET REPORTS AND COMMERCIAL PUBLICATIONS

Objection

• *I object. The document is an out-of-court statement and is therefore hearsay.*

Response

• *This statement is admissible as a market report or commercial publication pursuant to Rule 803(17). I have shown the document is a market quotation, tabulation, list, directory, or other published compilation that is generally used and relied upon by the public or persons in particular occupations.*

Cross-Reference to Colorado Rule 803(17)

Colorado cases have found the Kelley Blue Book to be a reliable market report, *People v. Thornton*, 251 P.3d 1147 (Colo. App. 2010), while the website drugs.com is not. *People v. Hard*, 2014 COA 132.

Explanation

Market reports or commercial publications are out-of-court statements that compile facts or data used by either the general public or by persons in particular professions or occupations and that are relied upon for the purposes of carrying out their daily businesses.

HEARSAY EXCEPTION: MARRIAGE, BAPTISM, AND SIMILAR CERTIFICATES

Objection

• *I object. The document is an out-of-court statement offered for its truth and is hearsay.*

Responses

• *This statement is admissible as a marriage, baptismal, or similar certificate pursuant to Rule 803(12). I have shown through the testimony of* (insert name of witness) *that:*

  » *this is a statement of fact contained in a certificate that shows the maker performed a marriage or other similar ceremony,* and

  » *was made by a clergyman, public official, or other person authorized by law or the practices of a religious organization to perform the act certified,* and

  » *which purports to be issued at the time of the act or within a reasonable time thereafter.*

Cross-Reference to Colorado Rule 803(12)

In criminal cases, admission of Rule 803(12) records does not implicate the confrontation clause, because such records are non-testimonial and the individual can be cross-examined. *People v.*

Hinojos-Mendoza, 140 P.3d 30 (Colo. App. 2006), *rev'd on other grounds*, 169 P.3d 662 (2007).

Explanation

Examples of facts that could be proved by the use of Rule 803(12) are paternity through a baptismal certificate and marriage through a marriage certificate.

HEARSAY EXCEPTION: OTHER EXCEPTIONS

Objections
- *I object. The question calls for a hearsay answer.*
- *I move to strike the answer as hearsay.*

Responses
- *The statement is admissible pursuant to the residual exception to the hearsay rule contained in Rule 807. I have shown through the testimony of* (insert name of witness) *that:*

  » *the statement is not specifically covered by any of the enumerated hearsay exceptions, and*

  » *the statement has circumstantial guarantees of trustworthiness equivalent to that of the enumerated exceptions, and*

  » *the statement is offered as evidence of a material fact, and*

  » *the statement is more probative on the point for which it is offered than any other evidence which I can procure through reasonable efforts, and*

  » *the general purposes of these rules in the interests of justice will be best served by the admission of this statement into evidence, and*

- *I have given the adverse parties notice sufficiently in advance of trial or hearing of my intention to offer the statements so as to afford them a fair opportunity to prepare to meet it.*

• *The statement is admissible pursuant to C.R.S. § 13-25-129 and is a statement of a child who witnessed or was a victim of sexual assault, incest, child abuse, or neglect and the court has determined, at an in camera hearing, that the time, content, and circumstances of the statement provide sufficient safeguards of reliability.*

Cross-Reference to Colorado Rules 807 and C.R.S. § 13-25-129

Admission of a Rule 807 statement requires 1) the statement be supported by circumstantial guarantees of trustworthiness; 2) the statement be offered as evidence of material facts; 3) the statement is more probative on the points for which it is offered than any other evidence that could be reasonably procured; 4) the general purposes of the rules of evidence and the interests of justice are best served by the admission of the statement; and 5) the adverse party had adequate notice in advance of trial of the intention of the proponent of the statement to offer it into evidence. *Vasquez v. People*, 173 P.3d 1099 (Colo. 2007).

Colorado has approved the admission of foreign, non-routine business records that had indicia of trustworthiness under the residual exception to the hearsay rule. *Hock v. New York Life Ins. Co.*, 876 P.2d 1242 (Colo. 1994).

In a criminal case, the admission of Rule 807 and C.R.S. § 13-25-129 evidence implicates the Sixth Amendment Confrontation Clause. *People v. Moreno*, 160 P.3d 242, 245 (Colo. 2007); *People v. Phillips*, 315 P.3d 136 (Colo. App. 2012). However, a defendant's confrontation rights are not violated by the admission of child hearsay under section C.R.S. § 13-25-129, where the child testified and the defendant cross-examined him. *People v. Ujaama*, 2012 COA 36.

G
H

Explanation

The residual exceptions to the hearsay rule provide identical catchall provisions that permit the admission of hearsay where, although not fitting any of the enumerated exceptions, the proffered hearsay possesses guarantees of trustworthiness equivalent to that of the enumerated exceptions and is more probative of the fact for which it is offered than any other available, admissible evidence.

Hearsay Exception: Present Sense Impression

Objections

- *I object. The question calls for a hearsay answer.*
- *I move to strike the answer as hearsay.*

Response

- *This statement is admissible as a present sense impression pursuant to Rule 803(1). I have shown through the testimony of* (insert name of witness) *that the statement describes or explains an event or condition and was made while the declarant was perceiving the event or condition.*

Cross-Reference to Colorado Rule 803(1)

Colorado requires that the present sense impression declaration be made while actually perceiving the event or condition. *People v. Czemerynski*, 786 P.2d 1100 (Colo. 1990). Statements made immediately thereafter are not admissible. *People v. Franklin*, 782 P.2d 1202 (Colo. App. 1989). In a criminal case, admission of present sense impressions against the defendant implicates the Sixth Amendment. *People v. Garrison*, 109 P.3d 1009 (Colo. App. 2005); *Davis v. Washington*, 126 S.Ct. 2266 (2006).

Explanation

A present sense impression is an out-of-court statement that describes or explains an occurrence or condition made at the time the declarant was perceiving the occurrence or condition, or immediately thereafter. The event described in the statement need not be exciting or startling. The guarantee of reliability for this hearsay exception is spontaneity or contemporaneity.

G
H

Hearsay Exception: Public Records and Reports

Objections

- *I object. The question calls for a hearsay answer.*

- *I move to strike the answer as hearsay.*

- (criminal cases only) *I object. The report is not admissible against a criminal defendant.*

Responses

- *The out-of-court statement is admissible as a public record or report pursuant to Rule 803(8). I have shown through the testimony of* (insert name of witness) *that:*

  - » *the document is a record, report, statement, or data compilation of a public office or agency setting forth the activities of the office or agency, or*

  - » *the record is of a public office or agency setting forth matters observed pursuant to duty imposed by law as to which matters there was a duty to report.*

Cross-Reference to Colorado Rule 803(8)

Even if administrative law judge's (ALJ) order was a public record, the proponent must establish that it contained factual findings, and ALJ's summary of offered evidence was not admissible under 803(8) nor any other exception to the hearsay rule. *Leiting v. Mutha*, 58 P.3d 1049 (Colo. App. 2002). Rule 803(8)'s

G
H

exception for public records and reports would include judgments of acquittal, mittimus, booking records, and driver's licenses. *Kinney v. People*, 187 P.3d 548 (Colo. 2008); *People v. Warrick*, 284 P.3d 139 (Colo. App. 2011); *People v. Vásquez*, 155 P.3d 588 (Colo. App. 2006). In the majority of circumstances, where the reports are ministerial, the confrontation clause is not implicated because the reports are non-testimonial. *People v. Warrick*, 284 P.3d 139 (Colo. App. 2011). In a civil case, as an official publication, the county attorney's website is self-authenticating, see CRE 902(5), and its statements setting forth the activities of the office fall within the exception to the hearsay rule of Rule 803(8). *Shook v. Pitkin County Board of County Commissioners*, 2015 COA 84.

Explanation

Such public records and reports are admissible unless the source of information or other circumstances indicate a lack of trustworthiness in the making or keeping of such records or reports. These records or reports gain their reliability from the public duty or the duty imposed by law which accompanies the maker's obligation to observe and record events. Records otherwise qualifying for admission pursuant to this exception are not admissible in a criminal case against the defendant when they are matters reported by law enforcement authorities. *People v. Clark*, 370 P.3d 197 (2015).

HEARSAY EXCEPTION:
RECORDED RECOLLECTION

Objections

- *I object. The question calls for a hearsay answer.*
- *I move to strike the answer as hearsay.*

Response

- *This statement is admissible as recorded recollection pursuant to Rule 803(5). I have shown through the testimony of* (insert name of witness) *that it is a memorandum or record concerning a matter about which a witness has knowledge, and was made or adopted by the witness when the matter was fresh in the witness's memory and reflects that knowledge correctly.*

Cross-Reference to Colorado Rule 803(5)

Unlike the federal rule, CRE 803(5) does not require that the witness have a current lack of memory. *People v. Rosenthal*, 670 P.2d 1254, 1256 (Colo. App. 1983). The time delay between the events described and a memorandum's creation has to be reasonable, which can be as long as two to three years. *People v. Miranda*, 2014 COA 102.

Explanation

Past recollection recorded must be distinguished from present recollection refreshed. Present recollection refreshed under Rule 612 presents no hearsay problem at all. Present recollection refreshed refers to a situation where a witness has a failure of memory. The witness is then shown the item that serves to refresh his or her recollection; the item is then removed from the witness, and the witness testifies from a refreshed recollection. Past recollection recorded refers to a document created by the witness, or at the witness's direction, when the matter was fresh in the witness's mind so as to accurately reflect that knowledge. The document may only be read to the jury, and may not be received as an exhibit, unless offered by the opponent. See *People v. Clary*, 950 P.2d 657 (Colo. App. 1997), for distinction between CRE 612 and 803(5).

G
H

HEARSAY EXCEPTION: RECORDS OF DOCUMENTS AFFECTING AN INTEREST IN PROPERTY

Objection

• *I object. The document is an out-of-court statement offered for its truth and is therefore hearsay.*

Response

• *The statement is admissible as a record of a document affecting an interest in property pursuant to Rule 803(14). I have shown through the testimony of* (insert name of witness) *that this is a record of a public office, and an applicable statute authorizes the recording of documents of that kind in such office.*

Cross-Reference to Colorado Rule 803(14)

The admission of Rule 803(14) records does not implicate the confrontation clause, because such records are non-testimonial and the individual can be cross-examined. *People v. Hinojos-Mendoza,* 140 P.3d 30 (Colo. App. 2006), *rev'd on other grounds,* 169 P.3d 662 (2007).

Explanation

A record of a document affecting an interest in property is an out-of-court writing that either relates to or establishes interest in property. It must be shown to be kept in an office that has the statutory authority to keep such records.

Hearsay Exception: Records of Regularly Conducted Activity (Business Records)

Objections

• *I object. The question calls for a hearsay answer.*

• *I move to strike the answer as hearsay.*

Responses

• *This statement is admissible as a business record pursuant to Rule 803(6). I have shown through the testimony of* (insert name of witness) *who is a custodian of the records, or person who has knowledge of the recordkeeping system, that the statement is contained in a:*

(for manually entered records)

   » *memorandum, report, record, or data compilation,*

   » *recording acts, events, conditions, opinions, or diagnoses,*

   » *made at or near the time the acts or events took place,*

   » *by or from information transmitted by one with personal knowledge of the event or act, where such record is kept in the course of regularly conducted business activities, and it was the regular practice of the business to make such a record.*

(for computer-generated records, repeat the above steps and add:)

> » *the computer and the program produce accurate results,*
> » *the computer was in good working order at relevant times with input procedures accurate, and*
> » *the computer operator possessed the knowledge and training to correctly operate the computer.*

Cross-Reference to Colorado Rule 803(6)

In certain circumstances, records of a third party may be admissible when integrated into the business records of another. Those circumstances include the use of standard form, or when other records are incorporated into those of business and/ or relied upon the business. *Schmutz v. Bolles*, 800 P.2d 1307 (Colo. 1990); *compare People v. NTB*, 2019 COA 150 (cloud-based files like Dropbox).

The business record exception includes computer records, but an additional foundation is required when the data is entered manually, rather than automatically. *People v. Huehn*, 52 P.3d 733 (Colo. App. 2002).

Authentication can be established by affidavit setting forth the evidentiary foundational requirements under Rule 803(6). *Henderson v. Master Klean Janitorial*, 70 P.3d 612 (Colo. App. 2003); *but see People v.*

Glover, 363 P.3d 736 (Colo. App. 2015) (Facebook pages). The custodian of record's lack of personal knowledge goes to weight, not admissibility. *In Re Fritzler*, 2017 COA 4 (Colo. App. 2017). Under certain circumstances, judicial notice can supply the foundational requirements. *People v. Marciano*, 2014 COA 92.

In criminal cases, business records are generally non-testimonial for constitutional for federal Confrontation Clause purposes, *Melendez-Diaz v. Massachusetts*, 557 U.S. 305 (2009).

Explanation

A record of regularly conducted activity, known in the common law as a business record, is a writing or compilation of data that records activities or happenings, including opinions, made in the course of a regularly conducted activity, and kept in the course of such activity, and created by and from a person with personal knowledge of the contents of the record, at or near the time of the event recorded. The exception covers records of regularly conducted activities on the part of all entities, whether or not they are formed for the purpose of making a profit.

HEARSAY EXCEPTION: RECORDS
OF RELIGIOUS ORGANIZATIONS

Objection

- *I object. The record is an out-of-court statement offered for its truth and is hearsay.*

Response

- *This statement is admissible as a record of a religious organization pursuant to Rule 803(11). I have shown through the testimony of* (insert name of witness) *that the statement is one of personal or family history and is contained in a regularly kept record of a religious organization.*

Cross-Reference to Colorado Rule 803(11)

Explanation

This rule creates a hearsay exception for records of personal and family history so long as such records are maintained in a regularly kept record of some religious organization.

Hearsay Exception: Records of Vital Statistics

Objection

• *I object. The record is an out-of-court statement offered for its truth and is hearsay.*

G
H

Response

• *The out-of-court statement is admissible as a record of a vital statistic pursuant to Rule 803(9) in that it is a record regarding a vital statistic that records a report made to a public office required by law to keep such records.*

Cross-Reference to Colorado Rule 803(9) Explanation

As with other out-of-court writings that are offered pursuant to a hearsay exception, records of vital statistics must be authenticated either through the testimony of the public officer who creates and maintains the records or, more easily, by the proffer of a certified copy of the public record pursuant to Rule 902(4).

Hearsay Exception: Reputation as to Character

Objections

- *I object. The question calls for a hearsay answer.*
- *I move to strike the answer as hearsay.*

Response

- *This statement is admissible as reputation as to character pursuant to Rule 803(21). I have shown through the testimony of* (insert name of witness) *that this is a statement of reputation of a person's character within the witness's community.*

Cross-Reference to Colorado Rule 803(21)

The reputation evidence must be based upon witness's own perception in community. *Lombardi v. Graham*, 794 P.2d 610 (Colo. 1990); *People v. Rowe*, 837 P.2d 260 (Colo. App. 1992), *rev'd on other grounds, Rowe v. People*, 856 P.2d 486 (Colo. 1993).

Explanation

Reputation is a collection of hearsay. Reputation of a person's character found among his or her associates in a community is admissible as a hearsay exception, subject to the relevance requirements of Rules 404, 405, and 608.

HEARSAY EXCEPTION: REPUTATION CONCERNING BOUNDARIES OR GENERAL HISTORY

Objections

- *I object. The question calls for a hearsay answer.*
- *I move to strike the answer as hearsay.*

G
H

Responses

- *This statement is admissible as a statement of reputation concerning boundaries or general history pursuant to Rule 803(20). I have shown through the testimony of* (insert name of witness) *that:*
  - » *this statement is a statement of reputation in a community,*
  - » *arising before the controversy, as to boundaries of, or customers affecting, lands in the community,* or
  - » *as to events of general history important to the community or state or nation in which located.*

Cross-Reference to Colorado Rule 803(20)

Explanation

Reputation concerning boundaries or general history involves a collection of hearsay drawn from a community regarding events of general import or knowledge in that community. The exception gains reliability from the force of general community knowledge.

Hearsay Exception: Reputation Concerning Personal or Family History

Objections

- *I object. The question calls for a hearsay answer.*
- *I move to strike the answer as hearsay.*

Response

- *The statement is admissible as a statement of reputation concerning personal or family history pursuant to Rule 803(19). I have shown through the testimony of* (insert name of witness) *that this is a statement of reputation among family members of one's family* (or among one's associates, or in the community), *concerning a person's adoption, birth, marriage, divorce, death, legitimacy, relationship by blood, adoption, or marriage, ancestry, or other similar fact of personal or family history.*

Cross-Reference to Colorado Rule 803(19)

Explanation

The witness who testifies concerning the reputation clearly must be familiar with that reputation that is shown by 1) the witness being a member of the relevant family, community, or group of associates, and by 2) the witness's familiarity with the reputation, having either heard it discussed or taken part in such discussions.

Hearsay Exception: Requirement of Unavailability for Rule 804 Hearsay Exceptions

Objections

- *I object. The question calls for a hearsay answer.*
- *I move to strike the answer as hearsay.*

Responses

- *The out-of-court statement meets* (insert the appropriate 804(b) exception).

- *The declarant is unavailable because the declarant:*

  » *is exempted from testifying concerning the subject of the statement by ruling from the court on the ground of privilege, or*

  » *persists in refusing to testify concerning the subject of the statement despite a court order to do so, or*

  » *testifies to a lack of memory on the subject of the statement, or*

  » *is unavailable to testify at the hearing because of death or illness, or*

  » *is absent from the hearing and I have been unable to procure his* (her) *attendance through process or other means, or*

  » (provide any other reason for the witness's absence).

Cross-Reference to Colorado Rule 804(a), (b)

There must be an actual demonstration of unavailability. *People v. Rosenthal*, 670 P.2d 1254 (Colo. 1983); *People v. Barnum*, 23 P.3d 1237 (Colo. App. 2001), *aff'd*, 53 P.2d 646 (Colo. 2002). When counsel asserts unavailability because the witness is absent from hearing, the proponent must demonstrate a good faith effort to procure attendance without success. *People v. Walters*, 765 P.2d 616 (Colo. App. 1988); *People v. Couillard*, 131 P.3d 1146 (Colo. App. 2005). A declarant's status as a co-defendant in a joint trial renders him or her unavailable for the purposes of CRE 804(a). *People v. Reed*, 216 P.3d 55 (Colo. App. 2008). A finding of unavailability under Rule 804(a) can also be the predicate for a victim of sexual assault, fifteen years old or younger, to testify via video deposition. *People in Interest of S.X.M.*, 271 P.3d 1124, 1129 (Colo. App. 2011).

Explanation

Note: Unavailability of a hearsay declarant does not, in and of itself, create an exception to the hearsay rule. Unavailability is merely the first requirement for all Rule 804 exceptions to the hearsay rule. The types of unavailability listed in Rule 804(a) are not the exclusive circumstances of unavailability. Rather,

---

this rule lists circumstances that *per se* amount to unavailability but fails to exclude any other legitimate showing of unavailability which the trial judge determines acceptable pursuant to Rule 804.

HEARSAY EXCEPTION: RESIDUAL EXCEPTION

Objections

- *I object. The question calls for a hearsay answer.*
- *I move to strike the answer as hearsay.*

G
H

Responses

- *The statement is admissible pursuant to the residual exception to the hearsay rule contained in Rule 807. I have shown through the testimony of* (insert name of witness) *that:*

  » *the statement is not specifically covered by any of the enumerated exceptions, and*

  » *the statement has circumstantial guarantees of trustworthiness equivalent to that of the enumerated exceptions, and*

  » *the statement is offered as evidence of a material fact, and*

  » *the statement is more probative on the point for which it is offered than any other evidence that I can procure through reasonable efforts, and*

  » *the general purposes of these rules in the interests of justice will be best served by the admission of this statement into evidence, and*

  » *I have given the adverse parties notice sufficiently in advance of trial or hearing of my intention to offer the statements so as to afford them a fair opportunity to prepare to meet it,* and

» *the witness is unavailable if offered under Rule 807.*

Cross-Reference to Colorado Rule 807

Admission of a Rule 807 statement requires 1) the statement be supported by circumstantial guarantees of trustworthiness; 2) the statement be offered as evidence of material facts; 3) the statement is more probative on the points for which it is offered than any other evidence which could be reasonably procured; 4) the general purposes of the rules of evidence and the interests of justice are best served by the admission of the statement; and 5) the adverse party had adequate notice in advance of trial of the intention of the proponent of the statement to offer it into evidence. *Vasquez v. People,* 173 P.3d 1099 (Colo. 2007).

Colorado has approved the admission of foreign, non-routine business records that had indicia of trustworthiness under the residual exception to the hearsay rule. *Hock v. New York Life Ins. Co.,* 876 P.2d 1242 (Colo. 1994).

In a criminal case, the admission of Rule 807 and C.R.S. § 13-25-129 evidence implicates the Sixth Amendment Confrontation Clause. *People v. Moreno,* 160 P.3d 242, 245 (Colo. 2007); *People v. Phillips,* 315 P.3d 136 (Colo. App. 2012). However, a defendant's confrontation rights are not violated by the admission of child hearsay under C.R.S. § 13-25-129, where the child testified and the defendant cross-examined him. *People v. Ujaama*, 2012 COA 36.

Explanation

The residual exceptions to the hearsay rule provide catchall provisions that permit the admission of hearsay where the proffered hearsay, although not fitting any of the enumerated exceptions, possesses guarantees of trustworthiness equivalent to that of the enumerated exceptions and is more probative of the fact for which it is offered than any other available, admissible evidence.

HEARSAY EXCEPTION: STATEMENT AGAINST INTEREST

Objections

- *I object. The question calls for a hearsay answer.*
- *I move to strike the answer as hearsay.*

Responses

- *This statement is admissible as a statement against interest pursuant to Rule 804(b)(3). I have shown through the testimony of* (insert name of witness) *that the statement was made by a declarant who is now unavailable pursuant to Rule 804(a),* and

  » *was at the time of its making, so far contrary to the declarant's pecuniary or proprietary interest,* or

  » *so far tended to subject the declarant to criminal or civil liability,* or

  » *to render invalid a claim by the declarant against another,* and

  » *that a reasonable person in the declarant's position would not have made this statement unless he* (she) *believed it to be true,* and

  » *in a criminal case corroborating circumstances clearly indicate the trustworthiness of the statement when the statement tends to expose the declarant to criminal liability.*

Cross-Reference to Colorado Rule 804(b)(3)

The rule was revised in 2011, consistent with recent amendments to FRE 804(b)(3), only to clarify that corroborating circumstances are required regardless of whether a statement is offered to inculpate or exculpate an accused. *See People v. Newton*, 966 P.2d 563 (Colo. 1998) (prosecutors seeking to admit statements against the accused must satisfy the corroboration requirement solely by reference to the circumstances surrounding the making of the statement). In determining trustworthiness, the court should consider when and where the statement was made, what prompted the statement, how the statement was made, and the substance of the statement, the nature and character of the statement, the relationship between the parties to the statement, the declarant's probable motivations for making the statement, and the circumstances under which the statement was made and whether the statement is really inculpatory. *People v. Valles*, 2013 COA 84; *People v. Beller*, 2016 COA 183. If the test for admission is satisfied, both the inculpatory and related collaterally neutral portions of the statement should be received, "unless the statement was so self-serving as to be unreliable, or unless the declarant had a significant motivation to curry favorable treatment such that the entire narrative should be excluded." *Nicholls v. People*, 2017 COA 71.

Explanation

In a criminal case, the admission of 804(b) (3), statements against interest evidence, implicates the Sixth Amendment Confrontation Clause. *Nicholls v. People*, 2017 COA 71; *Crawford Washington*, 541 U.S. 36 (2004); *Davis v. Washington*, 126 S.Ct. 2266 (2006).

G
H

HEARSAY EXCEPTION: STATEMENT IN ANCIENT DOCUMENTS

Objections

- *I object. The question calls for a hearsay answer.*
- *I move to strike the answer as hearsay.*

Response

- *This statement is admissible as a statement contained in an ancient document pursuant to Rule 803(16). I have shown through the testimony of* (insert name of witness) *that the statement is contained in a document in existence twenty years or more, the authenticity of which is established.*

Cross-Reference to Colorado Rule 803(16)

Ninety-four-old newspaper article found to be ancient document. *Timroth v. Oken*, 62 P.3d 1042 (Colo. App. 2002), *rev'd on other grounds, Board of Commissioners of Pitkin County v. Timroth*, 87 P.3d 102 (Colo. 2004).

Explanation

The foundational requirements for establishing authenticity of an ancient document require the condition of the document to create no suspicion regarding its authenticity, the document must have been kept in a place where it likely would be kept if it were authentic, and it must indeed have been in existence for at least twenty years at the time of its proffer at trial.

Hearsay Exception: Statement in Documents Affecting an Interest in Property

Objections

- *I object. The question calls for a hearsay answer.*
- *I move to strike the answer as hearsay.*

Responses

- *This statement is admissible pursuant to Rule 803(15) as a statement in a document affecting an interest in property. I have shown through the testimony of* (insert name of witness) *that:*
  - » *the statement is contained in a document purporting to establish or affect an interest in property,*
  - » *the matter stated was relevant to the purpose of the document,* and
  - » *the dealings with the property since the document was made have not been inconsistent with the truth of the statement or the purpose of the document.*

Cross-Reference to Colorado Rule 803(15)

Explanation

The requirements for qualification of admissibility under this rule are as follows. First, the factual statement contained in the document must relate to or be relevant to the purpose of the document. Second, the document would only be admissible so long as the dealings with the property have not been inconsistent with the truth of the statement or the purport of the document that was offered.

G
H

Hearsay Exception: Statement of Personal or Family History

Objections

- *I object. The question calls for a hearsay answer.*
- *I move to strike the answer as hearsay.*

Responses

- *This statement is admissible as a statement of personal or family history pursuant to Rule 804(b)(4). I have shown through the testimony of* (insert name of witness) *that:*

  » *the declarant is now unavailable pursuant to Rule 804(a), and the statement concerns the declarant's own birth, adoption, marriage, divorce, legitimacy, relationship by blood, adoption, or marriage, ancestry or other similar fact of personal or family history, even though the declarant had no means of acquiring personal knowledge of the matter stated, or*

  » *the statement concerns the foregoing matters, as well as the death of another person, where the declarant was related to the other person by blood, adoption, or marriage, or was so intimately associated with the other's family as to be likely to give accurate information concerning the matter declared.*

Cross-Reference to Colorado Rule 804(b)(4)

CRE 804(b)(4) excepts statements concerning matters of pedigree such as date of birth from the hearsay rule and statement concerning another's birth date is admissible, if he or she is related to the declarant by marriage. *People v. Buhrle*, 744 P.2d 747 (Colo. 1987).

Explanation

Note that the requirement of declarant's personal knowledge, which ordinarily must be apparent from the circumstances of the making of a declarant's admissible hearsay statement, is explicitly dispensed with pursuant to Rule 804(b)(4).

G
H

Hearsay Exception: Statement for Purposes of Medical Diagnosis or Treatment

Objections

- *I object. The question calls for a hearsay answer.*
- *I move to strike the answer as hearsay.*

Responses

- *This statement is admissible as a statement for purposes of medical diagnosis or treatment pursuant to Rule 803(4). I have shown through the testimony of* (insert name of witness) *that:*

  » *the statement was made for purposes of medical diagnosis or treatment, and was made for describing medical history,* or

  » *for describing past or present symptoms, pain, or sensations,* or

  » *for describing the inception or general character of the cause or external source thereof and was reasonably pertinent to diagnosis or treatment.*

Cross-Reference to Colorado Rule 803(4)

The statements must be reasonably related to the purpose of diagnosis and relied upon by the expert in formulating an opinion. *King v. People*, 785 P.2d 596 (Colo. 1990). The declarant must appreciate the purpose for which statements are made. *Oldsen v. People*, 732 P.2d 1132 (Colo. 1986). While statements of fault or identification of the perpetrator of assault are generally not admissible under Rule 803(4), an exception exists where the treatment provider perceives that the statement is necessary to treat the patient. *People v. Allee*, 77 P.3d 831 (Colo. App. 2003). CRE 803(4) is intended to include, within the hearsay exception, a party's statement to a non-treating physician for purposes of diagnosis in connection with pending litigation. *Kelly v. Haralampopoulos*, 327 P.3d 255 (Colo. 2014); *People v. Interest of ER*, 2018 COA 58. In criminal cases, statements under 803(4) implicate the confrontation clause. *People v. Vigil*, 127 P.3d 916 (Colo. 2006).

Explanation

Statements made to persons other than those immediately able to render medical assistance can qualify for this hearsay exception if made for purposes of obtaining medical diagnosis or treatment. However, statements of causation or the external source of the physical condition mentioned in the out-of-court statement will only be admissible if pertinent to the medical diagnosis or treatment. The key inquiry is whether the statement is pathologically germane to the diagnosis or treatment of a medical patient. Where and how an injury occurs is usually germane; who caused the injury usually is not.

Hearsay Exception: Statement Under Belief of Impending Death

Objections

- *I object. The question calls for a hearsay answer.*
- *I move to strike the answer as hearsay.*

Responses

- *The statement is one made under belief of impending death pursuant to § 13-25-119, C.R.S. (2016). I have shown through the testimony of* (insert name of witness) *that the statement:*
  - » *was made by a declarant who is now dead,* and
  - » *was made by the declarant while believing that his or her death was imminent,* and
  - » *concerns the cause or circumstances of what the declarant believed to be his or her impending death,* and
  - » *the statement was voluntary and the declarant was of sound mind,* and
  - » *the statement was not in response to leading questions.*

Cross-Reference to Colorado Rule 804(b)(2)

Colorado has a statute on dying declarations, not a rule. *See* C.R.S. § 13-25-119. The statute allows the admission of these statements in all proceedings when the declarant has died and it is established that 1) the declarant was conscious of approaching death and believed there was no hope of recovery at the time of the statement; 2) the statement was voluntary; 3) the statement was not the product of questioning calculated to elicit a particular response; and 4) the declarant was of sound mind. To render a dying declaration admissible, it is not necessary that the declarant should have stated that at the time it was made under a sense of impending death; it is enough if it satisfactorily appears that death was impending. *People v. Lagunas,* 710 P.2d 1145 (Colo. App. 1985).

Explanation

The statute requires a declarant to die as a foundational requirement to the offering of a statement under belief of impending death. The guarantee of reliability is found in the reasonable belief on the part of the declarant that he or she is about to die.

Hearsay Exception: Then-Existing Mental or Emotional Condition

Objections

- *I object. The question calls for a hearsay answer.*
- *I move to strike the answer as hearsay.*

Responses

- *This statement is admissible as a statement of a then-existing mental or emotional condition pursuant to Rule 803(3). I have shown through the testimony of* (insert name of witness) *that the statement:*
  - » *is of the declarant's then-existing state of mind, emotions, or sensation,* and
  - » *does not include a statement of memory or belief offered to prove the fact remembered or believed,* or
  - » *is intent to do an act in the future,*
  - » *even though a statement of memory or belief relates to the execution, revocation, identification, or terms of declarant's will.*

Cross-Reference to Colorado Rule 803(3)

Current statements of intent, plan, motive, design, mental feeling, pain, and bodily health are exceptions to the hearsay rule. *Pena v. People*, 173 P.3d 1107, 1113 (Colo. 2007). The statements can be made in response to a question. *People v. Acosta*, 2014 COA 82. Under a

Confrontation Clause analysis, the state of mind exception is a firmly rooted exception to the hearsay rule and under certain circumstances can be non-testimonial. *People v. Phillips*, 315 P.3d 136 (Colo. App. 2012).

Explanation

It is critical to note that only statements regarding a present mental or emotional condition fit within the exception. A statement regarding a past mental or emotional condition will not be admissible because there is no substantial guarantee of reliability, except when the statement relates to the declarant's will. Statements of a plan to do something in the future are considered statements of the mental condition of intent. *People v. McGrath*, 793 P.2d 664 (Colo. App. 1989). Statements of the victim's fear of defendant are admissible, if relevant. *People v. Robles*, 302 P.3d 269, 277–78 (Colo. App. 2011); *People v. Evans*, 987 P.2d 945 (Colo. App. 1998).

Hearsay Exception: Then-Existing Physical Condition

Objections

- *I object. The question calls for a hearsay answer.*
- *I move to strike the answer as hearsay.*

Response

- *This statement is admissible as a statement of a then-existing physical condition pursuant to Rule 803(3). I have shown through the testimony of* (insert name of witness) *that the statement is of the declarant's then-existing physical condition.*

Cross-Reference to Colorado Rule 803(3)

A victim's statements to a police officer describing physical injuries resulting from a sexual assault were admissible under CRE 803(3). *Pena v. People*, 173 P.3d 1107 (Colo. 2007). A victim's statement that his ears hurt in response to direct questioning by a teacher's aide was admissible as a then-existing physical condition under CRE 803(3). *People v. Phillips*, 2012 COA 176.

Under a Confrontation Clause analysis, the state-of-mind exception is a firmly rooted exception to the hearsay rule and under certain circumstances can be non-testimonial. *People v. Phillips*, 315 P.3d 136 (Colo. App. 2012).

Explanation

A statement of a then-existing physical condition gains its reliability from the contemporaneity of the statement and the existence of the physical condition described by the declarant. It is critical to note that only statements regarding present physical condition come within the exception. A statement regarding a past condition will not be admissible because there is no substantial guarantee of reliability.

IMPEACHMENT: BIAS, PREJUDICE, INTEREST, AND IMPROPER MOTIVE

Objections

- (for questions posed on cross-examination) *I object. Counsel is attempting to impeach the witness on improper grounds. The testimony that counsel is attempting to elicit is irrelevant.*

- (to extrinsic evidence) *I object. Counsel has not laid the proper foundation for use of extrinsic evidence to impeach. The witness whom counsel is attempting to impeach has not yet been called as a witness, or was not confronted with the alleged bias, interest, or improper motive on cross-examination.*

Responses

- (for objections posed on cross-examination) *I am attempting to show that the witness is biased* (or prejudiced, or has an interest in the outcome of the case, or has an improper motive for giving testimony).

- (for an objection posed to extrinsic evidence where the witness with the alleged bias, etc., has not yet been called to testify) *The witness has been listed as a witness by my opponent, and I offer it as evidence conditionally to avoid recalling the witness presently on the stand.*

- (for an objection posed to extrinsic evidence where the witness with the alleged bias, etc., has already testified) *I confronted* (insert name of witness) *with his* (her) *bias, etc., during cross-examination when I asked* (insert question), *and he* (she) *denied it.*

Cross-Reference to Colorado Rule

There is no Colorado Rule that specifically deals with bias, prejudice, interest, or improper motive. These are traditional areas of impeachment that fall within the general impeachment provision of Rule 607.

Explanation

Bias, prejudice, interest, and improper motive are particularly fertile areas for impeachment and are probably the most typical areas of impeachment with most witnesses. They all depend on the relationship of the witness with one of the parties or the subject of the litigation. *Merritt v. People*, 842 P.2d 162 (Colo. 1993); *People v. Trujillo*, 749 P.2d 441 (Colo. App. 1987). Use of pending charges to show motive or bias. *Kinney v. People*, 187 P.3d 548 (Colo. 2008); *compare People v. Caldwell*, 43 P.2d 663 (Colo. 2001). Gang membership is relevant to show motive, the circumstances surrounding the crime, or reluctance to testify or change in testimony. *People v. Clark*, 2015 COA 32; *People v. James*, 117 P.3d 91 (Colo. App. 2005). The court has admitted witness's fear of the defendant to explain a change in statement. *People v. Banks*, 2012 COA 157. Evidence that the defendant's expert and the defendant's insurer had a substantial connection was probative of bias and not barred by Rule 411. *Bonser v. Shainholtz*, 3 P.3d 422 (Colo. 2000); *Settle v. Basinger*, 2013 COA 18; *but see Garcia v. Mekonnen*, 156 P.3d 1171 (Colo. App. 2007) (clarifies substantial connection and Rule 403 applies).

I
J
K

IMPEACHMENT: CHARACTER EVIDENCE

Objections

- *I object. The character witness has insufficient knowledge of the witness's character to give an opinion.*

- *I object. The character witness has insufficient knowledge of the witness's reputation for dishonesty to give reputation testimony.*

Response

- *A foundation has been laid to demonstrate the character witness's sufficient familiarity with the witness's character for dishonesty* (or the witness's reputation for honesty in the community).

Cross-Reference to Colorado Rule 608(a)

Character evidence should be based upon the witness's own familiarity of the impeached individual or their reputation. *Lombardi v. Graham*, 794 P.2d 610 (Colo. 1990); *People v. Rowe*, 837 P.2d 260 (Colo. App. 1992), *rev'd on other grounds, Rowe v. People*, 856 P.2d 486 (Colo. 1993). By testifying, a party does not automatically place their character for truthfulness at issue. *People v. Miller*, 890 P.2d 84 (Colo. 1995). Rule 608(a) permits reputation and opinion evidence for truthful character only when the witness's truthful character is attacked. Pointing out inconsistencies in two stories is an insufficient foundation to elicit truthful character testimony. *People v. Wheatley*, 805 P.2d 1148 (Colo. App. 1990). A witness or party may not comment on another's truthfulness on a particular occasion. *Venalonzo v. People*, 2017 COA 9; *People v. Penn*, 2016 CO 32; *Liggett v. People*, 135 P.3d 725, (Colo. 2006); *People v. Relaford*, 2016 COA 99. Nor may an expert testify that children tend not to fabricate sexual contact. *People v. Wittrein*, 221 P.3d 1076 (Colo. 2009).

Under Rule 608(b), specific instances of untruthfulness may be inquired into on cross-examination, in the court's discretion. *People v. Distel*, 759 P.2d 654 (Colo. 1988). Untruthfulness has an expansive definition to include any dishonest conduct. *People v. Segovia*, 196 P.3d 1126 (Colo. 2008) (shoplifting); *People v. Campos*, 2015 COA 47 (using false SSN); *Leaf v. Beihoffer*, 2014 COA 117 (failure to file tax return). Only the underlying circumstances surrounding the conduct—not the fact of a criminal conviction itself—are admissible under the rule. *People v. Wellborne*, 428 P.3d 602 (Colo. App. 2017). Extrinsic evidence is not admissible to prove the specific instances of untruthfulness. *People v. Caldwell*, 43 P.3d 663 (Colo. App. 2001). However, where the evidence is being offered as impeachment by contradiction, extrinsic evidence is admissible. *People v. Hall*, 107 P.3d 1073 (Colo. App. 2004); *People v. Thomas*, 2014 COA 64.

Explanation

A witness may be impeached by opinion or reputation testimony that the witness has bad character for honesty. Once a witness has been impeached by evidence of dishonest character, such witness may be rehabilitated by the calling of a character witness who will testify as to the witness's character for honesty or truthfulness by way of opinion or reputation evidence. Expert testimony on character is prohibited under Rules 405(a) and 608(a).

I
J
K

IMPEACHMENT: MEMORY

Objection

- *I object. The question seeks to elicit irrelevant information. The question involves improper impeachment.*

Response

- *The question calls for an answer that will show the witness's inability to perceive. This is proper cross-examination.*

Cross-Reference to Colorado Rule

There is no Colorado Rule that specifically deals with impeachment regarding the ability to perceive. *See* Rule 607. However, psychiatric conditions and drug usage are admissible if it can be demonstrated that the impaired mental condition could affect perception or recollection. *People v. Borrelli*, 624 P.2d 900 (Colo. App. 1980) (psychiatric condition); *People v. McFee*, 2016 COA 97 (finding of incompetency three years previously too remote); *Paris v. Dance*, 194 P.3d 44 (Colo. App. 2008) (alcohol consumption on day in question); *Settle v. Basinger*, 2013 COA 18 (alcohol usage); *People v. Roberts*, 553 P.2d 93 (Colo. 1976) (drug usage); *People v. Lopez*, 2016 COA 179. It is improper to use willingness to take polygraph to bolster credibility). *People v. Muniz*, 190 P.3d 774 (Colo. App. 2008); *In Re G.E.S.*, 2016 COA 183 (improper to offer refusal to take polygraph).

Explanation

A witness may be impeached by showing an impaired ability to perceive the events in question. Such impeachment is typically accomplished by showing the time, place, and circumstances in which the perception occurs, from which the lawyer can argue and the jury can infer that the witness is not worthy of belief. Matters of perception include the ability to see, hear, smell, or feel some particular matter or item in question.

I
J
K

IMPEACHMENT: PRIOR CONVICTIONS

Objections

- (in a civil case) *I object. The proffered conviction is not a felony conviction within five years.*
- (in a criminal case) *I object. The probative value of this twenty-year-old felony conviction is outweighed by its prejudicial effect.*
- (in a criminal case) *I object. The conviction is not a felony.*

Responses

- *The proffered conviction is a felony conviction punishable within five years.*
- *Rule 403 does not prohibit the use of felony convictions as impeachment in criminal cases or in civil cases, when the conviction is within five years.*
- *The defendant opened the door by* (state reasons).

Cross-Reference to Colorado Rule

There is no Colorado Rule of Evidence 609. Statutes provide for impeachment by felony conviction in a civil case if the conviction is within five years from date of testimony. In criminal cases, there is no time limitation. C.R.S. § 13-90-101. The court has no discretion to prohibit impeachment by felony conviction. *People v. Diaz*, 985 P.2d 83 (Colo. App. 1999)

(Rule 403 does not apply). Generally, the scope of the impeachment inquiry is limited to the charge, date, and whether the conviction is by plea or trial and a brief inquiry into the circumstances. *People v. Lane*, 343 P.3d 1019 (Colo. App. 2014) Juvenile adjudications are not convictions and cannot be used under C.R.S. § 13-90-101. *State v. Corson*, 2016 CO 33. If a defendant is impeached based on a prior felony conviction, the trial court must instruct the jury that the defendant's prior felony conviction is to be considered only in evaluating the defendant's credibility. *People v. Mckeel*, 246 P.3d 638 (Colo. 2010).

Explanation

Colorado statutes control the use of felony convictions for impeachment in civil and criminal cases. Case law permits the introduction of misdemeanor arrests and convictions when the defendant opens the door. *People v. Pennese*, 830 P.2d 1085 (Colo. App. 1991); *People v. Mershon*, 844 P.2d 1240 (Colo. App. 1992), *aff'd and rev'd on other grounds*, *People v. Mershon*, 874 P.2d 1025 (Colo. 1994).

IMPEACHMENT: PRIOR INCONSISTENT STATEMENTS

Objections

- *I object. The proffered statement is not inconsistent with the witness's testimony and is irrelevant.*
- (in civil case) *I object. There has been a lack of foundation to ask this witness about any prior inconsistent statement.*
- (in civil case) *I object. There has been insufficient foundation for the admission of extrinsic evidence of any inconsistent statement.*
- (in criminal case) *I object. There has been an insufficient foundation for the admission of the inconsistent statement.*

Responses

- *The witness has testified during direct examination that* (insert testimony), *and this statement is inconsistent with the thrust of the direct testimony.*
- (in civil case) *The witness has been asked about the time, place, occasion when, and to whom the statement was made.*
- (in civil case) *During testimony, the declarant denied* (or did not remember) *making the prior inconsistent statement.*

- (in criminal case) *The witness was given an opportunity to deny or explain the statement* (or is available for recall) *and the statement relates to a matter in the personal knowledge of the witness.*

Cross-Reference to Colorado Rule 613

Colorado's procedure for admission of prior inconsistent statements for impeachment is substantially different than that used in federal court.

Explanation

In criminal cases, the use of prior inconsistent statements as substantive and impeachment evidence is initially controlled by statute, C.R.S. § 16-10-201. *Montoya v. People*, 740 P.2d 992 (Colo. 1987); *Davis v. People*, 310 P.3d 58, footnote 2 (Colo. 2013); *People v. Candelaria*, 107 P.3d 1080 (Colo. App. 2005), *rev'd on other grounds*, 148 P.3d 178 (Colo. 2006). In criminal cases, evidence of a prior inconsistent statement is admissible when the witness is given an opportunity to admit or deny the statement or the witness is available for recall and the statement is within the personal knowledge of the witness. *People v. Komar*, 2015 COA 171; *People v. Saiz*, 32 P.3d 441 (Colo. App. 2001). If the proponent cannot meet the foundational requirements of the statute, counsel can use Rule 613 to admit prior inconsistent statements to impeach. *Montoya v. People*, 740 P.2d 992 (Colo. 1987).

In civil cases, impeachment by prior inconsistent statement is governed by Rule 613. *Burlington Northern v. Hood*, 802 P.2d 458 (Colo. 1991). Before asking a witness about a prior inconsistent statement, counsel must draw the witness's attention to the time, place, occasion when, and to whom the statement was made. Counsel can use the statement to lay this foundation. Extrinsic evidence is only admissible when the witness denies or does not recall making the statement. Extrinsic evidence must be offered if the defendant denies the statement. *People v. Sandoval-Candelaria*, 328 P.3d 193, 199 (Colo. App. 2011), *rev'd on other grounds*, 2014 CO 21.

IMPEACHMENT: SPECIFIC INSTANCES OF MISCONDUCT

Objections

- (to cross-examination) *I object. The specific instance of conduct does not show lack of truth-telling ability.*

- (to extrinsic evidence, written or oral) *I object. Extrinsic evidence of specific instances of conduct relating to truthfulness is not admissible.*

Response

- *The specific instance of conduct shows lack of truth-telling ability in that* (insert reason or testimony).

Cross-Reference to Colorado Rule 608(b)

In the court's discretion, the examiner may inquire about specific instances of truthfulness or untruthfulness. *People v. Williams,* 89 P.3d 492 (Colo. App. 2003). Incidents of shoplifting, theft, using a false Social Security number, and failing to file a tax return are probative of untruthfulness under CRE 608(b), because the conduct is dishonest. *People v. Segovia,* 196 P.3d 1126 (Colo. 2008); *People v. Campos,* 2015 COA 47 (using false SSN is untruthful); *Leaf v. Beihoffer,* 2014 COA 117 (failure to file tax return).

The examiner is bound by the witness's answer, *Rice v. Department of Corrections,* 950 P.2d 676 (Colo.

App. 1997), and no extrinsic evidence is admissible, unless the evidence is being offered as impeachment by contradiction on a non-collateral matter. *People v. Hall,* 107 P.3d 1073 (Colo. App. 2004); *People v. Thomas,* 2014 COA 64. An analysis of admission under CRE 608(b) requires consideration of Rule 403. *McGill v. DIA Parking,* 2016 COA 165.

Even though a juvenile adjudication cannot be used for impeachment under C.R.S. § 13-90-101, if the conduct is dishonest, it may be admissible under CRE 608(b). *State v. Corson,* 2016 CO 33.

Explanation

On cross-examination, specific instances of conduct that show, without reference to the subject matter of the lawsuit, that a witness is not a truth teller are admissible pursuant to Rule 608(b) in the court's discretion. Extrinsic evidence of instances of misconduct relating to honesty is not admissible, unless it is impeachment by contradiction.

Insurance Against Liability

Objection

- *I object that the proponent is offering evidence of liability insurance on the issue of negligence or other wrongful conduct, or to show the proper amount of damages. I move for a mistrial.*

Response

- *This evidence of liability insurance is not offered on the issue of negligence or damages, but to show ownership, agency, control, or bias, or some other purpose other than liability.*

Cross-Reference to Colorado Rule 411

Generally, an attorney's attempt to refer to insurance coverage or a lack thereof at trial is improper. *Lombard v. Colo. Outdoor Educ. Ctr.*, 266 P.3d 412, 415 (Colo. App. 2011). Evidence of insurance is admissible if offered to show bias or prejudice of a witness. *Evans v. Colorado Permanente, etc.*, 902 P.2d 867 (Colo. App. 1995). Evidence that the defendant's expert and the defendant's insurer had a substantial connection was probative of bias and not barred by CRE 411. *Bonser v. Shainholtz*, 3 P.2d 422 (Colo. 2000); *see also Settle v. Basinger*, 2013 COA 18 (clarifies substantial connection and 403 applies), *and Garcia v. Mekonnen*, 156 P.3d 1171 (Colo. App. 2007).

Explanation

Contrary to common belief, the mere mention of the defendant being insured against liability is not necessarily inadmissible, nor need it lead to a mistrial. Evidence of insurance generally is not admissible only on the issues of liability and the ability of a party to pay damages.

JUDICIAL NOTICE

Objection

• *I object to the court judicially noticing* (insert fact offered) *in that it is not generally known in this jurisdiction and/or it is open to dispute and not capable of ready and certain verification.*

Responses

• *Judicial notice of* (insert fact offered) *is appropriate because:*

» *the fact is generally known by people in this local jurisdiction and to require other proof would waste the time of the court,* or

» *it is capable of ready and certain verification, and I have provided the court with evidence that proves the existence of the fact.*

Cross-Reference to Colorado Rule 201

CRE 201 allows a court, "at any stage of the proceeding," to take judicial notice of adjudicative facts, so long as those facts are "not subject to reasonable dispute" and are "either (1) generally known within the territorial jurisdiction of the trial court or (2) capable of accurate and ready determination by resort to sources whose accuracy cannot reasonably be questioned." *People v. Stanley*, 170 P.3d 782 (Colo. App. 2007). The court may take judicial notice of court records, including that a person with the defendant's name appeared at a felony sentencing hearing. *People v. Sa'ra*, 117 P.3d 51 (Colo. App. 2005). Judicial notice of court records requires same parties and similar issues, but court cannot take judicial notice of a fact that is disputed. *Dauwe v. Musante*, 122 P.3d 15 (Colo. App. 2005). Appellate court can take judicial notice of its own records. *Harriman v. Cabela's, Inc.*, 371 P.3d 758 (Colo. App. 2016). Court can take judicial notice of a calendar date, an unquestioned law of mathematics, a term of office, even drugs that may impair judgment or slow reflexes. *Timm v. Reitz*, 30 P.3d 1252 (Colo. App. 2001).

Explanation

Where the court is provided with authoritative sources that prove the fact, judicial notice is mandatory. Judicial notice is not required unless counsel supplies the court with the specific facts that are the subject of the request. *Martinez v. R.T.D.*, 832 P.2d 1060 (Colo. App. 1992). The court may judicially notice an appropriate fact on its own motion. The opposing party has the right to be heard concerning the propriety of judicial notice. However, the court can take judicial notice whether requested or not. *Colorow Health Care, LLC v. Fischer*, 420 P.3d 259 (Colo. 2018).

LAY OPINION EVIDENCE

Objections

• *I object. The question calls for an opinion.*

• *I move to strike the answer because it is stated in the form of an opinion.*

Response

• *This is permissible opinion from a lay witness because it is rationally based on the perception of the witness and would help the trier of fact to understand the witness's testimony and determine a fact in issue in this lawsuit and is not based on scientific, technical, or other specialized knowledge subject to Rule 702.*

Cross-Reference to Colorado Rules 701 and 702

Colorado has admitted lay opinion testimony on disability percentage, *Pyles-Knudsen v. Board*, 781 P.2d 164 (Colo. 1989); property value, *In re Plummer*, 709 P.2d 1388 (Colo. 1985); jealousy and abusiveness, *People v. Hulsing*, 825 P.2d 1027 (Colo. 1991); speed, *People v. T.R.*, 860 P.2d 559 (Colo. App. 1993); self-defense, *People v. Collins*, 730 P.2d 293 (Colo. 1986); robbery attempt, *People v. Jones*, 907 P.2d 667 (Colo. App. 1995); ballistics testimony admitted as lay opinion when testimony limited to location of bullet holes and path of bullets, *People v. Caldwell*, 43 P.2d 663

(Colo. App. 2001); whether sex assault was consensual, *People v. Hoskay*, 87 P.3d 194 (Colo. App. 2003). The distinction between Rule 701's rationally based knowledge versus the specialized knowledge test of Rule 702 is sometimes difficult to perceive.

The determination of whether the proffered testimony is lay or expert testimony, the court must look to the basis for the opinion. *Venalonzo v. People*, 2017 CO 9, ¶ 23. Where the witness provides testimony that could be expected to be based on an ordinary person's experiences or knowledge, then the witness is offering lay testimony. *Id.* However, if the witness provides testimony that could not be offered without specialized experiences, knowledge, or training, then the witness is offering expert testimony. *Id.; Vigil v. People*, 2019 CO 105 (shoe print evidence-lay opinion); *Campbell v. People*, 443 P.3d 72 (results of Horizontal Gaze Nystagmus test is expert testimony); *People v. Ramos*, 2017 CO 6 (differentiating blood cast-off from blood transfer was expert testimony); *People v. Kubuugu*, 2019 CO 9 (opinion was expert that defendant exuded a metabolized alcohol odor that indicated that he had consumed alcohol prior to entering the apartment complex); *Romero v. People*, 393 P.3d 973 (Colo. App. 2017) (grooming behavior requires expert opinion testimony); *People v. Garrison*, 411 P.3d 270 (Colo. App. 2017) (collecting cases on whether particular police testimony is lay or expert).

Explanation

Lay opinion is generally allowed where its admission makes the jury's fact-finding easier and more accurate. A typical admissible lay opinion occurs where a witness provides an inference to the jury that takes the place of describing a series of perceptions which in common experience add up to a rather ordinary inference or characterization (e.g., testimony that someone looked happy, sad, confused, angry, etc.). The difference between lay and expert opinion is that lay opinion is a conclusion based upon perceptions and observations or a reasoning process used in everyday life, while an expert opinion relies upon specialized knowledge and/or training.

L
M
N

LEADING QUESTIONS

Objection

- *I object to the question as leading.*

Responses

- *The question does not suggest the answer to the witness.*
- *Leading questions are permitted on preliminary matters, or when necessary to develop the witness's testimony, or because the party is hostile, an adverse party, or identified with an adverse party.*

Cross-Reference to Colorado Rule 611(c)

Leading questions are permitted on direct examination as may be necessary to develop the witness testimony or to lay a foundation for the admission of an exhibit. *People v. Petschow*, 119 P.3d 495 (Colo. App. 2005). Defense counsel is entitled to ask leading questions on cross-examination, and often: "[a]leading question is just a statement disguised as a question." *Doumbouya v. County Court of Denver*, 224 P.3d 425 (Colo. App. 2009).

Rule 611(c) prohibits leading questions on direct examination except to develop the witness's testimony or foundational matters.

Explanation

A leading question is one which suggests the desired answer to the witness so that it puts the desired answer in the witness's mouth or is one which makes it unclear as to whether the witness or the lawyer is testifying.

L
M
N

Misquoting the Witness

Objection

- *I object. Counsel is misquoting the witness. The witness has testified to* (insert substance of witness's testimony).

Response

- *The witness previously testified to* (insert substance of witness's testimony).

Cross-Reference to Colorado Rule

There is no Colorado Rule that specifically covers forms of questions. The court has discretion to sustain the objection pursuant to Rule 611(a).

Explanation

This objection is designed to prevent opposing counsel from shading the testimony of the witness as it had previously been rendered. The objection can serve as a reminder to the witness to listen carefully to opposing counsel's questions before answering.

NARRATIVES

Objections

- *I object. The question calls for a narrative response.*
- *I object. The witness is testifying in the form of a narrative.*

Response

- *The witness is testifying to relevant and admissible matters.*

Cross-Reference to Colorado Rule

There is no Colorado Rule that specifically covers forms of questions. The court has discretion to sustain the objection pursuant to Rule 611(a).

Explanation

This objection seeks to prevent the situation where counsel is not provided with notice by the question as to potential objectionable testimony by a witness. The best tactic for objecting counsel is to state, at the bench, the reasons for the objection; that is, to prevent inadmissible evidence from being heard by the jury and possibly cemented by a motion to strike. At the first instance when the witness testifies to inadmissible evidence during the narrative, opposing counsel should move to strike, approach the bench, and ask the judge to reconsider the objection to testimony in a narrative form.

Non-Responsive Answers

Objection

- *I move to strike the answer of the witness as non-responsive.*

Responses

- (if the objection is made by questioning counsel) *The answer of the witness is responsive to the question. The question put to the witness was* (insert the form of the question).

- (if the objection is made by opposing counsel) *I accept the answer.*

Cross-Reference to Colorado Rule

There is no Colorado Rule that specifically covers forms of questions. The court has discretion to sustain the objection pursuant to Rule 611(a). There is nothing *per se* wrong with the admission into evidence of testimony that may be unresponsive, provided that testimony is relevant for some purpose. *People v. Maestas*, 517 P.2d 461 (Colo. 1973). Where an answer is both unresponsive and inadmissible testimony, it should be stricken.

Explanation

The objection of non-responsiveness belongs only to questioning counsel. Answers that exceed the scope of the question may be the subject of a motion to strike by opposing counsel on specific substantive grounds. Opposing counsel may also object to the testimony of a witness as testimony in a narrative form that is treated under "Narratives" in this text.

OBJECTIONS

(See specific objections under appropriate captions in this text for forms of objections.)

Responses

(See specific responses under appropriate captions in this text for forms of responses.)

Cross-Reference to Colorado Rule 103

Once the court has definitively ruled on the issue, it is not necessary to renew the objection. *Vista Resorts v. Goodyear*, 117 P.3d 60 (Colo. App. 2005). Colorado has held where a party has lost an *in limine* motion on impeachment evidence, that party still preserves the right to appeal, although the party pre-emptively offers the evidence—disagreeing with *Ohler v. United States*, 529 U.S. 753 (2000). *McGill v. DIA Parking*, 2016 COA 165; *see also Kelly v. Haralampopoulos*, 327 P.3d 255 (Colo. 2014).

Explanation

Generally, failure to object waives appellate consideration of any error in the admission of evidence at trial. Objections must state the specific ground for exclusion of evidence unless the ground for objection is obvious. Objections must be timely in that they must be stated as soon as the objectionable nature of the question or answer becomes apparent.

OFFERS OF PROOF

Forms of the Offer

Ask the witness to state for the record, outside the hearing of the jury, what the witness's testimony would have been if the judge had not excluded it.

Cross-Reference to Colorado Rules 103(a)(2), 103(b)

The offer of proof must sufficiently inform the court of the nature and substance of the proposed evidence both to enable the trial court to exercise its discretion under the rules of evidence and to provide a basis for appellate review. *Iten v. Ungar*, 17 P.3d 129 (Colo. 2000). Typically, an offer of proof typically states 1) what the anticipated testimony of the witness would be if the witness were permitted to testify concerning the matter at issue; 2) the purpose and relevance of the testimony sought to be introduced; and 3) all the facts necessary to establish the testimony's admissibility. *People v. Weiss*, 133 P.3d 1180 (Colo. 2006).

O
P
Q

Explanation

The offer of proof must be made to preserve error when the court's ruling excludes evidence. The offer of proof must be made outside the hearing of the jury at the time of the sustaining of an objection, or it will be waived. The theory behind this rule is to provide the trial judge with the most informed opportunity to make the proper ruling.

O
P
Q

ORIGINAL DOCUMENT RULE
(BEST EVIDENCE RULE)

Objection

- *I object to the proponent's offer to show the contents of a writing by the use of secondary evidence.*

Responses

- *The terms of the writing are not an issue in the lawsuit, and thus the original is not required. The writing is offered to prove* (state reason).

- *The original's absence has been sufficiently accounted for and the secondary evidence is admissible because:*

  » *the original has been shown to have been lost or destroyed, not at the behest of my client,* or

  » *the original cannot be obtained by any available judicial process or procedure,* or

  » *the original is in the possession of an opposing party against whom the contents are offered, that party has failed to produce it, and that party has been put on notice by pleadings or otherwise, that the contents would be the subject of proof at trial.*

Cross-Reference to Colorado Rules 1001–1002

The preference for originals, or so-called best evidence rule, is a rule of documentary evidence that requires an original, under some circumstances, to prove the contents of a document or recording. *See* CRE 1001–1002. It is a rule limiting the admission of copies rather than a rule requiring the admission of an original recording, and in any event, it has no application where the recorded events themselves, rather than the contents of the document recording them, are at issue. *People v. Saiz*, 32 P.3d 441 (Colo. 2001). The best evidence or original writing rule does not require production of a copy of the electronically executed agreement to the exclusion of all other proof of agreement to its terms. *Berenson v. USA Hockey, Inc.*, 338 P.3d 379 (Colo. App. 2013).

Explanation

The key to understanding the original document rule is that this rule applies where the facts contained in the document are directly in issue in the case and the facts do not exist independent of the document. Typical documents that fall within the rule are written contracts, leases, or wills when the lawsuit is about the existence or interpretation of those documents.

PAYMENT OF MEDICAL
AND SIMILAR EXPENSES

Objection

- *I object. This evidence is inadmissible as an offer to pay medical expenses.*

Response

- *This statement is admissible because it is not offered on the issue of liability.*

Cross-Reference to Colorado Rule 409

Admission of the defendant's statements that he was sorry defeats the benevolent purpose of CRE 409, not only by hindering offers to assist with medical expenses and to compromise disputes, and discourages simple expressions of sympathy, goodwill, and civil behavior. *Bonser v. Shainholtz*, 983 P.2d 162, (Colo. App. 1999), *rev'd on other grounds, Bonser v. Shainholtz*, 3 P.3d 422 (Colo. 2000).

Explanation

Evidence of offers to pay medical and similar expenses, or payments of the same, are excluded only on the issue of liability and can be offered for any other relevant purpose.

PRESUMPTIONS

Form of Motion

• *I move for a directed verdict on* (the fact presumed) *because my opponent failed to come forward with sufficient evidence to rebut it.*

Response

• *A directed verdict is inappropriate because we have produced sufficient evidence to rebut the presumption such that a reasonable juror could find for my client on this fact.*

Cross-Reference to Colorado Rule 301

A presumption is a fact that is automatically proved by the proof of some other fact. In Colorado, there are permissive inferences and mandatory rebuttable presumptions. *People v. Hoskin*, 2016 CO 63. A permissive inference "allows, but does not require, the trier of fact to infer the elemental fact of a crime from proof by the prosecution of the predicate fact on which the inference is based." *Jolly v. People*, 742 P.2d 891 (Colo. 1987). In civil actions and proceedings, the creation of a presumption forces the opponent to come forward with sufficient evidence to rebut or meet the presumed fact. A rebuttable presumption does not, however, shift the original burden of proof. *Krueger v. Ary*, 205 P.3d 1150 (Colo. 2009); *Board of Assessment*

Appeals v. Sampson, 105 P.3d 198 (Colo. 2005). Using mandatory rebuttable presumptions in criminal cases "raises serious due process concerns precisely because these evidentiary devices can have the effect of relieving the prosecution of its constitutionally mandated burden of proof." *People v. Hoskin*, 2016 CO 63; *Jolly v. People*, 742 P.2d 891 (Colo. 1987). Delivery and receipt of information, once it is shown to have been put in the U.S. mail with proper address, postage, and return address, is a common example of a presumption with the opponent having the ability to offer evidence to rebut the presumption of delivery and receipt. When a conflict exists, the presumption does not arise. *Campbell v. IBM Corp.*, 867 P.2d 77 (Colo. App. 1993). C.R.S. § 13-21-403 contains presumptions applicable to product liability cases.

Explanation

A presumption is a fact that is automatically proved by the proof of some other fact. In Colorado, there are permissive inferences and mandatory rebuttable presumptions. The validity of a presumption is determined by whether the case is civil or criminal.

Privileges

Objection

- *I object to the admission of this evidence on the ground that it is privileged pursuant to* (state the particular form of privilege).

Response

- *This evidence is admissible because it does not fall within the privilege, or if privileged, such privilege has been waived.*

Cross-Reference to Colorado Rule 501

Colorado Rule 501 provides that except as provided by constitution, state statutes, or court rule, no person has the right to refuse to be a witness, refuse to produce any object or writing, or prohibit another from so doing. The primary privileges are contained in C.R.S. § 13-90-107, which covers husband-wife, physician-patient, attorney-client, priest-penitent, accountant-client, public officers, qualified interpreters, confidential intermediaries, certain self-evaluations, and victim advocate-victim privileges. There is also a limited newsperson's privilege set forth in C.R.S. § 13-90-119.

In 2016, Colorado adopted CRE 502, which limited the extent of waivers for attorney-client and work product due to inadvertent disclosure or disclosure to agencies or in other proceedings.

Explanation

The person asserting the privilege must demonstrate the existence of same and that the communications are protected. *Losavio v. District Court*, 533 P.2d 32 (Colo. 1975). A guardian *ad litem* is not in an attorney-client relationship with the child, but does have the power to waive the therapist-patient privilege. *People v. Gabriesheski*, 262 P.3d 653 (Colo. 2011), and *L.A.N. v. L.M.B.*, 292 P.3d 942 (Colo. 2013). Waiver of the privilege may only be by the client and may be either ex-pressed or implied. *Bond v. District Court*, 682 P.2d 33 (Colo. 1984). Where there is an implied waiver, the burden is upon the person seeking to overcome the privilege. *Mountain States v. DiFede*, 780 P.2d 533 (Colo. 1988). Most Colorado privileges are bars to communications except the husband-wife privilege, which is also a testimonial bar. *Cummings v. People*, 785 P.2d 920 (Colo. 1990). Colorado has restricted the implied waiver doctrine as it relates to the filing of a personal injury lawsuit, which generally asks for emotional distress damages. *Alcon v. Spicer*, 113 P.3d 735 (Colo. 2005); *Weil v. Dillon Co.*, 109 P.3d 127 (Colo. 2005).

If a mental health treatment provider believes, using his or her professional judgment, that statements made by a patient during a therapy session threaten imminent physical violence against a specific person or persons, triggering a "duty to warn," the patient's threatening statements are not protected by the psychologist-patient privilege. *People v. Kailey*, 2014 CO 50.

To demonstrate that the patient consented to the release of privileged information, the opposing party establish by an evidentiary showing that the privilege holder expressly or impliedly has given up any claim of confidentiality, by injecting the patient's physical or mental condition into the case as the basis of a claim or an affirmative defense. *People v. Johnson*, 2016 COA 69.

C.R.S. § 12-36.5-104(10)(a) protects the records of a professional review committee from all forms of subpoena or discovery. The statute further protects the records from admissibility in civil suits. *Colorado Medical Board v. Office of Administrative Courts*, 333 P.3d 70 (2014).

Testimonial privileges are not barred by Sixth Amendment confrontation considerations. *People v. Turner*, 109 P.3d 639 (Colo. 2005). C.R.S. § 25-1-1202 lists sixty-five different statutes containing confidentiality or privilege protections.

Refreshing Present Recollection

Objections

- *I object to the attempt to refresh the witness's recollection in the absence of a demonstrated failure of memory.*
- *I object to the witness's reading from the exhibit used to refresh his (her) recollection because it is not in evidence and because it is hearsay.*

Responses

- *The witness has shown a failure of memory, and I am attempting to refresh his (her) recollection pursuant to Rule 612.*
- *The exhibit used to refresh the witness's recollection is already in evidence, and it is either not hearsay or the exhibit meets an exception to the hearsay rule.*

Cross-Reference to Colorado Rule 612

The court may require that the document be produced if used to refresh recollection before the witness testified. The adverse party may use the document for cross-examination and offer portions of the document that relate to the witness's testimony. Colorado cases have recognized the legal treatise statement that refreshing recollection is "a last-ditch means to secure information known to the witness but apparently lost to conscious memory." *J.S. v. Chambers*, 226 P.3d 1193, 1200 (Colo. App. 2009). Failure to produce

R
S

the document can result in striking the testimony or granting a mistrial. Rule 612 is not an exception to the hearsay rule but rather, a tool used to assist the witness's memory during examination. *People v. Clary,* 950 P.2d 667 (Colo. App. 1997) (explaining distinction between Rule 612 and Rule 803(5)).

Explanation

The steps in refreshing a witness's memory are as follows:

1) Establish the witness's failure of memory (full or partial).

2) Mark the refreshing document for identification.

3) Show the witness the refreshing document and ask the witness to read it silently.

4) Ask if the witness has read it.

5) Ask if the witness's memory is refreshed with respect to the forgotten fact.

6) Take the refreshing exhibit from the witness.

7) Re-ask the question that drew the original failure of memory.

Relevance: Generally

Objections

- *I object on the ground that the question calls for an irrelevant answer.*

- *I move to strike the answer as irrelevant.*

Response

- *The evidence is relevant because it has some tendency to make more likely a fact that is material to either a claim or defense in the lawsuit, or bears on the weight or credibility of a witness or of the evidence.*

Cross-Reference to Colorado Rules 401 and 402

The general directive of CRE 402 is that "[a]ll relevant evidence is admissible," unless the United States Constitution, the Colorado Constitution, a state statute, the evidence rules, or the Supreme Court prohibits that evidence. *Murray v. Just in Case Lighthouse, LLC,* 374 P.3d 443 (Colo. 2016).

In weighing the balancing test of probative value verses prejudicial effect attendant to Rule 403, the proffered evidence "should be given its maximal probative weight and its minimal prejudicial effect." *People v. District Court of El Paso County,* 869 P.2d 1281, 1285 (Colo. 1994). Thus, the evidentiary rules

R
S

strongly favor the admission of relevant, material evidence. *Palizzi v. City of Brighton,* 228 P.3d 957, 962 (Colo. 2010); *Herrera v. Lerma,* 2018 COA 141 (permanent impairment rating typically used in worker's compensation case is relevant and thus admissible in personal injury case and not excludable under CRE 403.

Explanation

Often, the terms "relevance" and "materiality" are used interchangeably. This is incorrect. Materiality has a more precise meaning than relevance and can be seen as being a term that is within the meaning of relevance. Materiality is the relationship between the proposition for which the evidence is offered and the issues in the case. If the evidence is offered to prove a proposition that is not a matter in issue, the evidence is said to be immaterial; relevancy includes both the test of materiality and something more. Relevancy is the tendency of the evidence in question to establish a material proposition. *See People v. Garcia,* 179 P.3d 250, 255 (Colo. App. 2007).

Relevance: Conditional Admissibility

Objections

- *I object. The proffered evidence is not relevant and admissible unless other facts are proved.*

- *I move to strike the conditionally admitted evidence of* (insert name of witness or evidence). *Counsel has failed to prove additional facts that are necessary to show the relevance of that conditionally admitted evidence.*

Responses

- *I will show the relevance of the proffered evidence by proof of the following additional facts through the testimony of* (insert name of witness).

- *The relevance of the conditionally admitted facts has been shown through the additional evidence given in the testimony of* (insert name of witness).

Cross-Reference to Colorado Rule 104(b)

In making CRE 104(b) determinations, the judge merely decides, as a preliminary matter, whether the foundation evidence is sufficient to support a reasonable finding by a jury of the fulfillment of the condition. If showing is made, the trial court admits the evidence for the jury's consideration. *People v. Brown*, 313 P.3d 608 (Colo. App. 2011). Only when the proffered evidence, considered in its total context, is manifestly insufficient to sustain a reasonable finding by the jury of the conditional fact should the evidence be inadmissible. *Burlington Northern R.R. Co. v. Hood*, 802 P.2d 458 (Colo. 1990). The court can require an offer of proof that will fulfill the necessary condition precedent to admissibility. *People v. Lyle*, 613 P.2d 896 (Colo. 1980).

Explanation

The judge is given a great deal of authority in making the preliminary findings necessary to determining the admissibility of evidence.

RELEVANCE: EXCLUSION OF RELEVANT EVIDENCE ON GROUNDS OF PREJUDICE, CONFUSION, OR WASTE OF TIME

Objections

- *I object on the ground that this evidence is inadmissible because its probative value is substantially outweighed by the prejudicial effect of the evidence.*
- *The introduction of this evidence will confuse the issue before the jury.*
- *The evidence is merely cumulative.*

Responses

- *The evidence is admissible because it is logically relevant under Rule 401, and:*
    - » *its probative value is not substantially outweighed by the danger of unfair prejudice,* or
    - » *any potential confusion of issues is easily cured by an instruction by the court,* or
    - » *the evidence is corroborative of an issue central to the case.*

Cross-Reference to Colorado Rule 403

Colorado has a five-factor test in balancing whether the probative value is substantially outweighed by the danger of unfair prejudice. Those factors are 1) the importance of the fact of consequence for which the evidence is offered; 2) the strength and length of inferences necessary to establish the fact of consequence; 3) the availability of other methods of proof; 4) whether the fact is being disputed; and 5) the utility of a limiting instruction. *Vialpando v. People*, 727 P.2d 1090 (Colo. 1990); *Yusem v. People*, 210 P.3d 458 (Colo. 2009). In making its decision, the trial court must maximize probative value and minimize prejudicial effect. *People v. District Court*, 869 P.2d 1281 (Colo. 1994).

Explanation

The balancing test of Rules 401 and 403 is tilted heavily in favor of the admissibility of logically relevant evidence or evidence with probative value, in that the prejudice must substantially outweigh the probative value in order to require exclusion.

R
S

Relevance: Limited Admissibility

Objections

- *I object. The question calls for irrelevant information on the issue* (insert the issue).

- *I object. I move that the court instruct the jury the answer is irrelevant and inadmissible on the issue* (insert the issue), *and I request a limiting instruction.*

- *I object. The question calls for irrelevant information as against my client.*

- *I object. I move the court instruct the jury the answer is irrelevant as to my client, and I request a limiting instruction.*

Responses

- *The evidence offered is relevant and admissible for all purposes and a limiting instruction is inappropriate.*

- *The evidence is relevant and admissible against all parties. A limiting instruction is inappropriate.*

Cross-Reference to Colorado Rule 105

Absent a special statutory requirement, a trial court is under no obligation to provide a limiting instruction without a specific request that it do so. *People v. Thomas*, 345 P.3d 959 (Colo. App. 2014); *People v. Griffin*, 224 P.3d 292 (Colo. App. 2009);

People v. Welsh, 80 P.3d 296 (Colo. 2003); *People v. Garcia*, 981 P.2d 214 (Colo. App. 1999); *Hansen v. Lederman*, 759 P.2d 810 (Colo. App. 1988). Failure to do so will allow consideration of the evidence for all purposes. However, in cases involving child sexual and physical abuse, similar transaction evidence, and child hearsay statements, the court must, *sua sponte*, give limiting instructions. C.R.S. § 16-10-301(3); C.R.S. § 13-25-129, C.R.S. (2016).

Explanation

In most situations, it is incumbent upon opposing counsel to seek limitation of the evidence to its proper admissible purpose by requesting a limiting instruction from the judge. For strategic reasons, such as an instruction will highlight unfavorable evidence, the opponent may forgo the right to a limiting instruction. Where statutes mandate the giving of a limited purpose instruction, the court has no discretion.

Relevance: Rule of Completeness

Objections

- *I object to the admissibility of the proffered writing* (or recording) *unless other portions of the writing* (or recording) *are also admitted. These other portions are necessary to explain or to put in context the proffered writing* (or recording).

- *I object to the admissibility of the proffered writing* (or recording) *unless other related writings* (or recordings) *are necessary to explain or to put in context the proffered writing* (or recording).

Response

- *The proffered statement* (or recording) *does not need explanation or context. Other portions of the statement* (or recording), *or additional writings* (or recordings), *are not necessary to a fair understanding of the proffered statement* (or recording).

Cross-Reference to Colorado Rule 106

Both the rule of completeness and the related concept of "opening the door," require that the proffered evidence be relevant and admission is necessary in fairness to not leave a misimpression with the jury. *People v. Melillo*, 25 P.3d 769 (Colo. 2001). The rule of completeness does not require the admission of the defendant's first video interview with police, because it was self-serving hearsay and untrustworthy. *People v. Davis*, 218 P.3d 718, 731 (Colo. App. 2008).

Explanation

The rule of completeness embodied in Rule 106 is essentially a rule of fairness. *People v. Wilson*, 841 P.2d 337 (Colo. App. 1992). Because the appearance of unfairness can seriously damage the credibility of the proponent, the rule of completeness should be anticipated by proffering counsel and every effort should be made to fairly show the appropriate context in which an offered statement or recording was made; *People v. Short*, 425 P.3d 1208 (Colo. App. 2018) (however, where the prosecution offers only part of defendant's statement without including the exculpatory portion and thus misleading the jury, the remainder of the statement should be received or none of the statement should be admitted).

SUBSEQUENT REMEDIAL MEASURES

Objection

• *I object. This is evidence of a subsequent remedial measure.*

Responses

• *This evidence is not offered on the issue of negligence or culpable conduct, but is offered to show notice, ownership, control, feasibility of precautionary measures, or impeachment.*

• *My opponent has "opened the door" to this evidence by his or her pleadings or the questioning of* (insert name of witness).

Cross-Reference to Colorado Rule 407

Federal Rule 407 was amended in 1997 to extend the exclusionary principle to subsequent remedial measures to product liability cases and to clarify that the rule applies only to remedial measures made after the occurrence that causes the damage giving rise to the action. Colorado did not adopt the federal 1997 changes.

C.R.S. § 13-21-404 limits subsequent scientific and technical advancements in product liability cases to duty-to-warn situations. The statute does not necessarily prohibit evidence of remedial actions that pre-exist the occurrence of the injury at issue. *Uptain v. Huntington Lab, Inc.*, 723 P.2d 1322 (Colo. 1986). Nor does the statute or Rule 407 prohibit introduction of subsequent remedial measures for impeachment purposes, *White v. Caterpillar*, 867 P.2d 100 (Colo. App. 1993), nor introduction of remedial action evidence to establish ownership or feasibility when controverted. *Martinez v. W. R. Grace*, 782 P.2d 827 (Colo. App. 1989). CRE 407 does not apply to product liability cases premised on design defect, but evidence of subsequent remedial measures must nevertheless pass muster under the general relevancy and balancing tests of CRE 401 and 403 and must be probative of the claimed defect. *Forma Scientific, Inc. v. Biosera*, 960 P.2d 908 (Colo. 1998).

Explanation

The reason for the evidentiary prohibition against subsequent remedial measures is to create an incentive for correction of defective conditions. Such evidence is *per se* inadmissible only on the issues of negligence or culpable conduct.

Colorado Rules of Evidence

As Adopted October 23, 1979
Effective January 1, 1980
Including Amendments through January 1, 2020

CONTENTS

ARTICLE VII. Opinions and Expert Testimony

ARTICLE VIII. Hearsay

ARTICLE I
GENERAL PROVISIONS

Rule 101. Scope

These rules govern proceedings in all courts in the State of Colorado, to the extent and with the exceptions stated in Rule 1101.

Rule 102. Purpose and Construction

These rules shall be construed to secure fairness in administration, elimination of unjustifiable expense and delay, and promotion of growth and development of the law of evidence to the end that the truth may be ascertained and proceedings justly determined.

Rule 103. Rulings on Evidence

(a) **Effect of erroneous ruling.** Error may not be predicated upon a ruling which admits or excludes evidence unless a substantial right of the party is affected, and

(1) **Objection.** In case the ruling is one admitting evidence, a timely objection or motion to strike appears of record, stating the specific ground of objection, if the specific ground was not apparent from the context; or

(2) **Offer of proof.** In case the ruling is one excluding evidence, the substance of the evidence was made known to the court by offer or was apparent from the context within which questions were asked.

Once the court makes a definitive ruling on the record admitting or excluding evidence, either at or before trial, a party need not renew an objection or offer of proof to preserve a claim of error for appeal.

(b) **Record of offer and ruling.** The court may add any other or further statement which shows the character of evidence, the form in which it was offered, the objection made, and the ruling thereon. It may direct the making of an offer in question and answer form.

(c) **Hearing of jury.** In jury cases, proceedings shall be conducted, to the extent practicable, so as to prevent inadmissible evidence from being suggested to the jury by any means, such as making statements or offers of proof or asking questions in the hearing of the jury.

(d) **Plain error.** Nothing in this rule precludes taking notice of plain errors affecting substantial rights although they were not brought to the attention of the court.

Source: (a) amended and adopted June 20, 2002, effective July 1, 2002.

Rule 104. Preliminary Questions

(a) **Questions of admissibility generally.** Preliminary questions concerning the qualification of a person to be a witness, the existence of a privilege, or the admissibility of evidence shall be determined by the court, subject to the provisions of subdivision (b). In making its determination it is not bound by the rules of evidence except those with respect to privileges.

(b) **Relevancy conditioned on fact.** When the relevancy of evidence depends upon the fulfillment of a condition of fact, the court shall admit it upon, or subject to, the introduction of evidence sufficient to support a finding of the fulfillment of the condition.

(c) **Hearing of jury.** Hearings on the admissibility of confessions shall in all cases be conducted out of the hearing of the jury. Hearings on other preliminary matters shall be so conducted when the interests of justice require or, when an accused is a witness, if he so requests.

(d) **Testimony by accused.** The accused does not, by testifying upon a preliminary matter, subject himself to cross-examination as to other issues in the case.

(e) **Weight and credibility.** This rule does not limit the right of a party to introduce before the jury evidence relevant to weight or credibility.

Rule 105. Limited Admissibility

When evidence which is admissible as to one party or for one purpose but not admissible as to another party or for another purpose is admitted, the court, upon request, shall restrict the evidence to its proper scope and instruct the jury accordingly.

Rule 106. Remainder of or Related Writings or Recorded Statements

When a writing or recorded statement or part thereof is introduced by a party, an adverse party may require him at that time to introduce any other part or any other writing or recorded statement which ought in fairness to be considered contemporaneously with it.

ARTICLE II
JUDICIAL NOTICE

Rule 201. Judicial Notice of Adjudicative Facts

(a) **Scope of rule.** This rule governs only judicial notice of adjudicative facts.

(b) **Kinds of facts.** A judicially noticed fact must be one not subject to reasonable dispute in that it is either (1) generally known within the territorial jurisdiction of the trial court or (2) capable of accurate and ready determination by resort to sources whose accuracy cannot reasonably be questioned.

(c) **When discretionary.** A court may take judicial notice, whether requested or not.

(d) **When mandatory.** A court shall take judicial notice if requested by a party and supplied with the necessary information.

(e) **Opportunity to be heard.** A party is entitled upon timely request to an opportunity to be heard as to the propriety of taking judicial notice and the tenor of the matter noticed. In the absence of prior notification, the request may be made after judicial notice has been taken.

(f) **Time of taking notice.** Judicial notice may be taken at any stage of the proceeding.

(g) **Instructing jury.** In a civil action or proceeding, the court shall instruct the jury to accept as conclusive any fact judicially noticed. In a criminal case, the court shall instruct the jury that it may, but is not required to, accept as conclusive any fact judicially noticed.

ARTICLE III
PRESUMPTIONS IN CIVIL ACTIONS AND PROCEEDINGS

Rule 301. Presumptions in General in Civil Actions and Proceedings

In all civil actions and proceedings not otherwise provided for by statute or by these rules, a presumption imposes upon the party against whom it is directed the burden of going forward with evidence to rebut or meet the presumption, but does not shift to such party the burden of proof in the sense of the risk of non-persuasion, which remains throughout the trial upon the party on whom it was originally cast.

Rule 302. (No Colorado Rule Codified)

ARTICLE IV
RELEVANCY AND ITS LIMITS

Rule 401. Definition of "Relevant Evidence"

"Relevant evidence" means evidence having any tendency to make the existence of any fact that is of consequence to the determination of the action more probable or less probable than it would be without the evidence.

Rule 402. Relevant Evidence Generally Admissible; Irrelevant Evidence Inadmissible

All relevant evidence is admissible, except as otherwise provided by the Constitution of the United States, by the Constitution of the State of Colorado, by these rules, or by other rules prescribed by the Supreme Court, or by the statutes of the State of Colorado. Evidence which is not relevant is not admissible.

Rule 403. Exclusion of Relevant Evidence on Grounds of Prejudice, Confusion, or Waste of Time

Although relevant, evidence may be excluded if its probative value is substantially outweighed by the danger of unfair prejudice, confusion of the issues, or misleading the jury, or by considerations of undue delay, waste of time, or needless presentation of cumulative evidence.

Rule 404. Character Evidence Not Admissible to Prove Conduct; Exceptions; Other Crimes

(a) **Character evidence generally.** Evidence of a person's character or a trait of his character is not admissible for the purpose of proving that he acted in conformity therewith on a particular occasion, except:

(1) **Character of accused.** In a criminal case, evidence of a pertinent trait of his character offered by an accused, or by the prosecution to rebut the same or if evidence of the alleged victim's character for aggressiveness or violence is offered by an accused and admitted under Rule 404(a)(2), evidence of the same trait of character of the accused offered by the prosecution;

(2) **Character of alleged victim.** In a criminal case, evidence of a pertinent trait of character of the alleged victim of the crime offered by an accused, or by the prosecution to rebut the same, or evidence of a character trait of peacefulness of the victim offered by the prosecution in a homicide case to rebut evidence that the alleged victim was the first aggressor;

(3) **Character of witness.** Evidence of the character of a witness as provided in Rules 607, 608, and § 13-90-101, C.R.S. (2016).

(b) **Other crimes, wrongs, or acts.** Evidence of other crimes, wrongs, or acts is not admissible to prove the character of a person in order to show that he acted in conformity therewith. It may, however, be admissible for other purposes, such as proof of motive, opportunity, intent, preparation, plan, knowledge, identity, or absence of mistake or accident, provided that upon request by the accused, the prosecution in a criminal case shall provide reasonable notice in advance of trial, or during trial if the court excuses pretrial notice on good cause shown, of the general nature of any such evidence it intends to introduce at trial.

Source: (a) amended and adopted June 20, 2002, effective July 1, 2002; (a)(1), (a)(2), and (b) amended and effective September 27, 2007.

Rule 405. Methods of Proving Character

(a) **Reputation or opinion.** In all cases in which evidence of character or a trait of character of a person is admissible, proof may be made by testimony as to reputation or by testimony in the form of an opinion. On cross-examination, inquiry is allowable into relevant specific instances of conduct.

(b) **Specific instances of conduct.** Except as limited by § § 16-10-301 and 18-3-407, in cases in which character or a trait of character of a person is an essential element of a charge, claim, or defense, proof may also be made of specific instances of that person's conduct.

Source: (b) amended September 29, 2005, effective January 1, 2006.

Rule 406. Habit; Routine Practice

Evidence of the habit of a person or of the routine practice of an organization, whether corroborated or not and regardless of the presence of eyewitnesses, is relevant to prove that the conduct of the person or organization on a particular occasion was in conformity with the habit or routine practice.

Rule 407. Subsequent Remedial Measures

When, after an event, measures are taken which, if taken previously, would have made the event less likely to occur, evidence of the subsequent measures is not admissible to prove negligence or culpable conduct in connection with the event. This rule does not require the exclusion of evidence of subsequent measures when offered for another purpose, such as proving ownership, control, or feasibility of precautionary measures, if controverted, or impeachment.

Rule 408. Compromise and Offers to Compromise

(a) **Prohibited uses.** Evidence of the following is not admissible on behalf of any party, when offered to prove liability for, invalidity of, or amount of a claim that was disputed as to validity or amount, or to impeach through a prior inconsistent statement or contradiction:

(1) furnishing or offering or promising to furnish accepting or offering or promising to accept a valuable consideration in compromising or attempting to compromise the claim; and

(2) conduct or statements made in compromise negotiations regarding the claim, except when offered in a criminal case and the negotiations related to a claim by a public office or agency in the exercise of regulatory, investigative, or enforcement authority.

(b) **Permitted uses.** This rule does not require exclusion if the evidence is offered for purposes not prohibited by subdivision (a). Examples of permissible purposes include proving a witness's bias or prejudice; negating a contention of undue delay; and proving an effort to obstruct a criminal investigation or prosecution.

Source: Entire rule amended and effective September 27, 2007.

Rule 409. Payment of Medical and Similar Expenses

Evidence of furnishing or offering or promising to pay medical, hospital, or similar expenses occasioned by an injury is not admissible to prove liability for the injury.

Rule 410. Offer to Plead Guilty; *Nolo Contendere*; Withdrawn Pleas of Guilty

Except as otherwise provided by statutes of the State of Colorado, evidence of a plea of guilty, later withdrawn, or a plea of *nolo contendere*, or of an offer to plead guilty or *nolo contendere* to the crime charged or any other crime, or of statements made in any connection with any of the foregoing pleas or offers, is not admissible in any civil or criminal action, case, or proceeding against the person who made the plea or offer. This rule shall not apply to the introduction of voluntary and reliable statements made in court on the record in connection with any of the foregoing pleas or offers where offered for impeachment purposes or in a subsequent prosecution of the declarant for perjury or false statement.

This rule shall be superseded by any amendment to the Colorado Rules of Criminal Procedure which is inconsistent with this rule, and which takes effect after the effective date of these Colorado Rules of Evidence.

Rule 411. Liability Insurance

Evidence that a person was or was not insured against liability is not admissible upon the issue whether he acted negligently or otherwise wrongfully. This rule does not require the exclusion of evidence of insurance against liability when offered for another purpose, such as proof of agency, ownership, or control, or bias or prejudice of a witness.

Rule 412. (No Colorado Rule Codified)

See § 18-3-407 and § 13-25-138, C.R.S.

ARTICLE V
PRIVILEGES

Rule 501. Privileges Recognized Only as Provided

Except as otherwise required by the Constitution of the United States, the Constitution of the State of Colorado, statutes of the State of Colorado, rules prescribed by the Supreme Court of the State of Colorado pursuant to constitutional authority, or by the principles of the common law as they may be interpreted by the courts of the State of Colorado in light of reason and experience, no person has a privilege to:

(1) Refuse to be a witness; or

(2) Refuse to disclose any matter; or

(3) Refuse to produce any object or writing; or

(4) Prevent another from being a witness or disclosing any matter or producing any object or writing.

Rule 502. Attorney-Client Privilege and Work Product; Limitations on Waiver

The following provisions apply, in the circumstances set out, to disclosure of a communication or information covered by the attorney-client privilege or work-product protection.

(a) **Disclosure Made in a Colorado Proceeding or to a Colorado Office or Agency; Scope of a Waiver.** When the disclosure is made in a Colorado proceeding or to an office or agency of a Colorado state, county, or local government and waives the attorney-client privilege or work product protection, the waiver extends to an undisclosed communication or information in a Colorado proceeding only if:

(1) the waiver is intentional;

(2) the disclosed and undisclosed communications or information concern the same subject matter; and

(3) they ought in fairness to be considered together.

(b) **Inadvertent Disclosure.** When made in a Colorado proceeding or to an office or agency of a Colorado state, county, or local government, the disclosure does not operate as a waiver in a Colorado proceeding if:

(1) the disclosure is inadvertent;

(2) the holder of the privilege or protection took reasonable steps to prevent disclosure; and

(3) the holder promptly took reasonable steps to rectify the error, including (if applicable) following C.R.C.P. 26(b)(5)(B).

(c) **Disclosure Made in a Federal or other State Proceeding.** When the disclosure is made in a proceeding in federal court or the court of another state and is not the subject of a court order concerning waiver, the disclosure does not operate as a waiver in a Colorado proceeding if the disclosure:

(1) would not be a waiver under this rule if it had been made in a Colorado proceeding; or

(2) is not a waiver under the law governing the state or federal proceeding where the disclosure occurred.

(d) **Controlling Effect of a Court Order.** A Colorado court may order that the privilege or protection is not waived by disclosure connected with the litigation pending before the court—in which event the disclosure is also not a waiver in any other proceeding.

(e) **Controlling Effect of a Party Agreement.** An agreement on the effect of disclosure in a Colorado proceeding is binding only on the parties to the agreement, unless it is incorporated into a court order.

(f) **Definitions.** In this rule:

(1) "attorney-client privilege" means the protection that applicable law provides for confidential attorney-client communications; and

ARTICLE VI
WITNESSES

Rule 601. General Rule of Competency

Every person is competent to be a witness except as otherwise provided in these rules, or in any statute of the State of Colorado.

Rule 602. Lack of Personal Knowledge

A witness may not testify to a matter unless evidence is introduced sufficient to support a finding that he has personal knowledge of the matter. Evidence to prove personal knowledge may, but need not, consist of the testimony of the witness himself. This rule is subject to the provisions of Rule 703, relating to opinion testimony by expert witnesses.

Rule 603. Oath or Affirmation

Before testifying, every witness shall be required to declare that he will testify truthfully, by oath or affirmation administered in a form calculated to awaken his conscience and impress his mind with his duty to do so.

Rule 604. Interpreters

An interpreter is subject to the provisions of these rules relating to qualification as an expert and the administration of an oath or affirmation that he will make a true translation.

Rule 605. Competency of Judge as Witness

The judge presiding at the trial may not testify in that trial as a witness. No objection need be made in order to preserve the point.

Rule 606. Competency of Juror as Witness

(a) **At the trial.** A member of the jury may not testify as a witness before that jury in the trial of the case in which the juror is sitting. No objection need be made in order to preserve the point.

(b) **Inquiry into validity of verdict or indictment.** Upon an inquiry into the validity of a verdict or indictment, a juror may not testify as to any matter or statement occurring during the course of the jury's deliberations or to the effect of anything upon his or any other juror's mind or emotions as influencing him to assent to or dissent from the verdict or indictment or concerning his mental processes in connection therewith. But a juror may testify about (1) whether extraneous prejudicial information was improperly brought to the jurors' attention, (2) whether any outside influence was improperly brought to bear upon any juror, or (3) whether there was a mistake in entering the verdict onto the verdict form. A juror's affidavit or evidence of any statement by the juror may not be received on a matter about which the juror would be precluded from testifying.

Source: Entire rule amended and effective and committee comment added and effective September 27, 2007.

Rule 607. Who May Impeach

The credibility of a witness may be attacked by any party, including the party calling him. Leading questions may be used for the purpose of attacking such credibility.

Rule 608. Evidence of Character and Conduct of Witness

(a) **Opinion and reputation evidence of character.** The credibility of a witness may be attacked or supported by evidence in the form of opinion or reputation, but subject to these limitations: (1) the evidence may refer only to character for truthfulness or untruthfulness, and (2) evidence of truthful character is admissible only after the character of the witness for truthfulness has been attacked by opinion or reputation evidence or otherwise.

(b) **Specific instances of conduct.** Specific instances of the conduct of a witness, for the purpose of attacking or supporting the witness's character for truthfulness, other than conviction of crime as provided in § 13-90-101, may not be proved by extrinsic evidence. They may, however, in the discretion of the court, if probative of truthfulness or untruthfulness, be inquired into on cross-examination of the witness (1) concerning his character for truthfulness or untruthfulness, or (2) concerning the character for truthfulness or untruthfulness of another witness as to which character the witness being cross-examined has testified.

The giving of testimony, whether by an accused or by any other witness, does not operate as a waiver of the accused or the witness's privilege against self-incrimination when examined with respect to matters that relate only to character for truthfulness.

Source: (b) amended September 29, 2005, effective January 1, 2006.

Rule 609. (No Colorado Rule Codified)

See § 13-90-101, C.R.S.

Rule 610. Religious Beliefs or Opinions

Evidence of the beliefs or opinions of a witness on matters of religion is not admissible for the purposes of showing that by reason of their nature his credibility is impaired or enhanced.

Rule 611. Mode and Order of Interrogation and Presentation

(a) **Control by court.** The court shall exercise reasonable control over the mode and order of interrogating witnesses and presenting evidence so as to (1) make the interrogation and presentation effective for the ascertainment of the truth, (2) avoid needless consumption of time, and (3) protect witnesses from harassment or undue embarrassment.

(b) **Scope of cross-examination.** Cross-examination should be limited to the subject matter of the direct examination and matters affecting the credibility of the witness. The court may, in the exercise of discretion, permit inquiry into additional matters as if on direct examination.

(c) **Leading questions.** Leading questions should not be used on the direct examination of a witness except as may be necessary to develop his testimony. Leading questions should be permitted on cross-examination. When a party calls a hostile witness, an adverse party, or a witness identified with an adverse party, interrogation may be by leading questions.

Rule 612. Writing Used to Refresh Memory

If a witness uses a writing to refresh his memory for the purpose of testifying, either—

---

(1) while testifying, or

(2) before testifying, if the court in its discretion determines it is necessary in the interests of justice, an adverse party is entitled to have the writing produced at the hearing, to inspect it, to cross-examine the witness thereon, and to introduce in evidence those portions which relate to the testimony of the witness. If it is claimed that the writing contains matters not related to the subject matter of the testimony the court shall examine the writing in camera, excise any portions not so related, and order delivery of the remainder to the party entitled thereto. Any portion withheld over objections shall be preserved and made available to the appellate court in the event of an appeal. If a writing is not produced or delivered pursuant to order under this rule, the court shall make any order justice requires, except that in criminal cases when the prosecution elects not to comply, the order shall be one striking the testimony or, if the court in its discretion determines that the interests of justice so require, declaring a mistrial.

Rule 613. Prior Statements of Witnesses

(a) **Examining witness concerning prior inconsistent statements for impeachment purposes.** Before a witness may be examined for impeachment by prior inconsistent statement the examiner must call the attention of the witness to the particular time and occasion when, the place where, and the person to whom he made the statement. As a part of that foundation, the examiner may refer to the witness statement to bring to the attention of the witness any purported prior inconsistent statement. The exact language of the prior statement may be given.

Where the witness denies or does not remember making the prior statement, extrinsic evidence, such as a deposition, proving the utterance of the prior evidence is admissible. However, if a witness admits making the prior statement, additional extrinsic evidence that the prior statement was made is inadmissible.

Denial or failure to remember the prior statement is a prerequisite for the introduction of extrinsic evidence to prove that the prior inconsistent statement was made.

Rule 614. Calling and Interrogation of Witnesses by Court

(a) **Calling by court.** The court may, on its own motion or at the suggestion of a party, call witnesses and all parties are entitled to cross-examine witnesses thus called.

(b) **Interrogation by court.** The court may interrogate witnesses, whether called by itself or by a party.

(c) **Objections.** Objections to the calling of witnesses by the court or to interrogation by it may be made at the time or at the next available opportunity when the jury is not present.

Rule 615. Exclusion of Witnesses

At the request of a party the court shall order witnesses excluded so that they cannot hear the testimony of other witnesses, and it may make the order of its own motion. This rule does not authorize exclusion of (1) a party who is a natural person, or (2) an officer or employee of a party which is not a natural person designated as its representative by its attorney, or (3) a person whose presence is shown by a party to be essential to the presentation of his cause.

ARTICLE VII
OPINIONS AND EXPERT TESTIMONY

Rule 701. Opinion Testimony by Lay Witnesses

If the witness is not testifying as an expert, the witness's testimony in the form of opinions or inferences is limited to those opinions or inferences which are (a) rationally based on the perception of the witness, (b) helpful to a clear understanding of the witness's testimony or the determination of a fact in issue, and (c) not based on scientific, technical, or other specialized knowledge within the scope of Rule 702.

Source: Entire rule amended and adopted June 20, 2002, effective July 1, 2002.

Rule 702. Testimony by Experts

If scientific, technical, or other specialized knowledge will assist the trier of fact to understand the evidence or to determine a fact in issue, a witness qualified as an expert by knowledge, skill, experience, training, or education may testify thereto in the form of an opinion or otherwise.

Rule 703. Bases of Opinion Testimony by Experts

The facts or data in the particular case upon which an expert bases an opinion or inference may be those perceived by or made known to the expert at or before the hearing. If of a type reasonably relied upon by experts in the particular field in forming opinions or inferences upon the subject, the facts or data need not be admissible in evidence in order for the opinion or inference to be admitted. Facts or data that are otherwise inadmissible shall not be disclosed to the jury by the proponent of the opinion or inference unless the court determines that their probative value in assisting the jury to evaluate the expert's opinion substantially outweighs their prejudicial effect.

Source: Entire rule amended and adopted June 20, 2002, effective July 1, 2002.

Rule 704. Opinion on Ultimate Issue

Testimony in the form of an opinion or inference otherwise admissible is not objectionable because it embraces an ultimate issue to be decided by the trier of fact.

Rule 705. Disclosure of Facts or Data Underlying Expert Opinion

The expert may testify in terms of opinion or inference and give reasons therefore without first testifying to the underlying facts or data, unless the court requires otherwise. The expert may in any event be required to disclose the underlying facts or data on cross-examination.

Rule 706. Court Appointed Experts

(a) **Appointment.** The court may on its own motion or on the motion of any party enter an order to show cause why expert witnesses should not be appointed, and may request the parties to submit nominations. The court may appoint any expert witnesses agreed upon by the parties, and may appoint expert witnesses of its own selection. An expert witness shall not be appointed by the court unless he consents to act. A witness so appointed shall be informed of his duties by the court in writing, a copy of which shall be filed with the clerk, or at a conference in which the parties shall have opportunity to participate. A witness so appointed shall advise the parties of his findings, if any; his deposition may be taken by any party; and he may be called to testify by the court or any party. He shall be subject to cross-examination by each party, including a party calling him as a witness.

(b) **Compensation.** Expert witnesses so appointed are entitled to reasonable compensation in whatever sum the court may allow. The compensation thus fixed is payable from funds which may be provided by law in criminal cases and civil actions and proceedings involving just compensation under the 5th Amendment. In other civil actions and proceedings the compensation shall be paid by the parties in such proportion and at such time as the court directs, and thereafter charged in like manner as other costs.

(c) **Disclosure of appointment.** In the exercise of its discretion, the court may authorize disclosure to the jury of the fact that the court appointed the expert witness.

(d) **Parties' experts of own selection.** Nothing in this rule limits the parties in calling expert witnesses of their own selection.

ARTICLE VIII
HEARSAY

Rule 801. Definitions

The following definitions apply under this article:

(a) **Statement.** A "statement" is (1) an oral or written assertion or (2) nonverbal conduct of a person, if it is intended by him to be communicative.

(b) **Declarant.** A "declarant" is a person who makes a statement.

(c) **Hearsay.** "Hearsay" is a statement other than one made by the declarant while testifying at the trial or hearing, offered in evidence to prove the truth of the matter asserted.

(d) **Statements Which Are Not Hearsay.** A statement is not hearsay if—

(1) **Prior statement by witness.** The declarant testifies at the trial or hearing and is subject to cross-examination concerning the statement, and the statement is (A) inconsistent with his testimony, or (B) consistent with his testimony and is offered to rebut an express or implied charge against him of recent fabrication or improper influence or motive, or (C) one of identification of a person made after perceiving him, or

(2) **Admission by party-opponent.** The statement is offered against a party and is (A) the party's own statement in either an individual or a representative capacity, or (B) a statement of which the party has manifested his adoption or belief in its truth, or (C) a statement by a person authorized by the party to make a statement concerning the subject, or (D) a statement by the party's agent or servant concerning a matter within the scope of the agency or employment, made during the existence of the relationship, or (E) a statement by a co-conspirator of a party during the course and in furtherance of the conspiracy. The contents of the statement shall be considered but are not alone sufficient to establish the declarant's authority under subdivision (C), the agency or employment relationship and scope thereof under subdivision (D), or the existence of the conspiracy and participation therein of the declarant and the party against whom the statement is offered under subdivision (E).

Source: (d)(2) amended and committee comment added November 25, 1998, effective January 1, 1999.

Rule 802. Hearsay Rule

Hearsay is not admissible except as provided by these rules or by the civil and criminal procedural rules applicable to the courts of Colorado or by any statutes of the State of Colorado.

Rule 803. Hearsay Exceptions: Availability of Declarant Immaterial

The following are not excluded by the hearsay rule, even though the declarant is available as a witness:

(1) **Spontaneous present sense impression.** A spontaneous statement describing or explaining an event or condition made while the declarant was perceiving the event or condition.

(2) **Excited utterance.** A statement relating to a startling event or condition made while the declarant was under the stress of excitement caused by the event or condition.

(3) **Then existing mental, emotional, or physical condition.** A statement of the declarant's then existing state of mind, emotion, sensation, or physical condition (such as intent, plan, motive, design, mental feeling, pain, and bodily health), but not including a statement of memory or belief to prove the fact remembered or believed unless it relates to the execution, revocation, identification, or terms of declarant's will.

(4) **Statements for purposes of medical diagnosis or treatment.** Statements made for purposes of medical diagnosis or treatment and describing medical history, or past or present symptoms, pain, or sensations, or the inception or general character of the

cause or external source thereof insofar as reasonably pertinent to diagnosis or treatment.

(5) **Recorded recollection.** A past recollection recorded when it appears that the witness once had knowledge concerning the matter and: (A) can identify the memorandum or record, (B) adequately recalls the making of it at or near the time of the event, either as recorded by the witness or by another, and (C) can testify to its accuracy. The memorandum or record may be read into evidence but may not itself be received unless offered by an adverse party.

(6) **Records of regularly conducted activity.** A memorandum, report, record, or data compilation, in any form, of acts, events, conditions, opinions, or diagnosis, made at or near the time by, or from information transmitted by, a person with knowledge, if kept in the course of a regularly conducted business activity, and if it was the regular practice of that business activity to make the memorandum, report, record, or data compilation, all as shown by the testimony of the custodian or other qualified witness, or by certification that complies with Rule 902(11), Rule 902(12), or a statute permitting certification, unless the source of information or the method or circumstances of preparation indicate lack of trustworthiness. The term "business" as used in this paragraph includes business, institution, association, profession,

occupation, and calling of every kind, whether or not conducted for profit.

(7) **Absence of entry in records kept in accordance with the provisions of paragraph (6).** Evidence that a matter is not included in the memoranda, reports, records, or data compilations in any form, kept in accordance with the provisions of paragraph (6), to prove the nonoccurrence or nonexistence of the matter, if the matter was of a kind of which a memorandum, report, record, or data compilation was regularly made and preserved, unless the sources of information or other circumstances indicate lack of trustworthiness.

(8) **Public records and reports.** Unless the sources of information or other circumstances indicate lack of trustworthiness, records, reports, statements, or data compilations, in any form, of public offices or agencies, setting forth (A) the activities of the office or agency, or (B) matters observed pursuant to duty imposed by law as to which matters there was a duty to report, excluding, however, in criminal cases matters observed by police officers and other law enforcement personnel, or (C) in civil actions and proceedings and against the Government in criminal cases, factual findings resulting from an investigation made pursuant to authority granted by law.

(9) **Records of vital statistics.** Records or data compilations, in any form, of births, fetal deaths, deaths, or marriages, if the report thereof was made to a public office pursuant to requirements of law.

(10) **Absence of a public record.** Testimony—or a certification under Rule 902—that a diligent search failed to disclose a public record or statement if: (A) the testimony or certification is admitted to prove that (i) the record or statement does not exist; or (ii) a matter did not occur or exist, if a public office regularly kept a record or statement for a matter of that kind; and (B) in a criminal case, a prosecutor who intends to offer a certification provides written notice of that intent at least 14 days before trial, and the defendant does not object in writing within 7 days of receiving the notice—unless the court sets a different time for the notice or the objection.

(11) **Records of religious organizations.** Statements of births, marriages, divorces, deaths, legitimacy, ancestry, relationship by blood or marriage, or other similar facts of personal or family history, contained in a regularly kept record of a religious organization.

(12) **Marriage, baptismal, and similar certificates.** Statements of fact contained in a certificate that the maker performed a marriage or other ceremony or administered a sacrament, made authorized by a

clergyman, public official, or other person by the rules or practices of a religious organization or by law to perform the act certified, and purporting to have been issued at the time of the act or within a reasonable time thereafter.

(13) **Family records.** Statements of fact concerning personal or family history contained in family Bibles, genealogies, charts, engravings on rings, inscriptions on family portraits, engravings on urns, crypts, or tombstones, or the like.

(14) **Records of documents affecting an interest in property.** The record of a document purporting to establish or affect an interest in property, as proof of the content of the original recorded or filed document and its execution and delivery by each person by whom it purports to have been executed, if the record is a record of a public office and an applicable statute authorizes the recording of documents of that kind in that office.

(15) **Statements in documents affecting an interest in property.** A statement contained in a document purporting to establish or affect an interest in property if the matter stated was relevant to the purpose of the document, unless dealings with the property since the document was made have been inconsistent with the truth of the statement or the purport of the document.

(16) **Statements in ancient documents.** Statements in a document in existence twenty years or more the authenticity of which is established.

(17) **Market reports, commercial publications.** Market quotations, tabulations, lists, directories, or other published compilations, generally used and relied upon by the public or by persons in particular occupations.

(18) **Learned treatises.** To the extent called to the attention of an expert witness upon cross-examination or relied upon by him in direct examination, statements contained in published treatises, periodicals, or pamphlets on a subject of history, medicine, or other science or art, established as a reliable authority by the testimony or admission of the witness or by other expert testimony or by judicial notice. If admitted, the statements may be read into evidence and may be received as exhibits, as the court permits.

(19) **Reputation concerning personal or family history.** Reputation among members of his family by blood, adoption, or marriage, or among his associates, or in the community, concerning a person's birth, adoption, marriage, divorce, death, legitimacy, relationship by blood, adoption, or marriage, ancestry, or other similar fact of his personal or family history.

(20) **Reputation concerning boundaries or general history.** Reputation in a community, arising

before the controversy, as to boundaries of or customs affecting lands in the community, and reputation as to events of general history important to the community or state or nation in which located.

(21) **Reputation as to character.** Reputation of a person's character among his associates or in the community.

(22) **Judgment of previous conviction.** Evidence of a final judgment, entered after a trial or upon a plea of guilty or nolo contendere, adjudging a person guilty of a crime punishable by death or imprisonment in excess of one year, to prove any fact essential to sustain the judgment, but not including, when offered by the Government in a criminal prosecution for purposes other than impeachment, judgments against persons other than the accused. The pendency of an appeal may be shown but does not affect admissibility.

(23) **Judgment as to personal, family, or general history or boundaries.** Judgments as proof of matters of personal, family, or general history, or boundaries, essential to the judgment, if the same would be provable by evidence of reputation.

(24) [Transferred to Rule 807]

Source: (24) added November 15, 1984, effective April 1, 1985; (24) transferred to Rule 807 and committee comment added, effective January 1, 1999; (6) amended and adopted June 20, 2002, effective July 1, 2002; (10) amended and adopted and (10) committee comment added and adopted, effective February 18, 2014.

Rule 804. Hearsay Exceptions: Declarant Unavailable

(a) **Definition of unavailability.** "Unavailability as a witness" includes situations in which the declarant—

(1) is exempted by ruling of the court on the ground of privilege from testifying concerning the subject matter of his statement; or

(2) persists in refusing to testify concerning the subject matter of his statement despite an order of the court to do so; or

(3) testifies to a lack of memory of the subject matter of his statement; or

(4) is unable to be present or to testify at the hearing because of death or then existing physical or mental illness or infirmity; or

(5) is absent from the hearing and the proponent of his statement has been unable to procure his attendance (or in the case of a hearsay exception under

subdivision (b)(3) or (4) his attendance or testimony)
by process or other reasonable means.

A declarant is not unavailable as a witness if his
exemption, refusal, claim of lack of memory, inability,
or absence is due to the procurement or wrongdoing
of the proponent of his statement for the purpose of
preventing the witness from attending or testifying.

(b) **Hearsay exceptions.** The following are not
excluded by the hearsay rule if the declarant is unavailable as a witness:

(1) **Former testimony.** Testimony given as a
witness at another hearing of the same or a different
proceeding, or in a deposition taken in compliance
with law in the course of the same or another proceeding, if the party against whom the testimony is
now offered, or, in a civil action or proceeding, a pre-
decessor in interest, had an opportunity and similar
motive to develop the testimony by direct, cross, or
redirect examination.

(2) (No Colorado Rule Codified.) See § 13-25-
119 C.R.S. (2016).

(3) **Statement against interest.**

A statement that:

(A) a reasonable person in the declarant's
position would have made only if the person

believed it to be true because, when made, it was so contrary to the declarant's proprietary or pecuniary interest or had so great a tendency to invalidate the declarant's claim against someone else or to expose the declarant to civil or criminal liability; and

(B) is supported by corroborating circumstances that clearly indicate its trustworthiness, if it is offered in a criminal case as one that tends to expose the declarant to criminal liability.

(4) **Statement of personal or family history.**

(A) A statement concerning the declarant's own birth, adoption, marriage, divorce, legitimacy, relationship by blood, adoption, or marriage, ancestry, or other similar fact of personal or family history, even though declarant had no means of acquiring personal knowledge of the matter stated; or (B) a statement concerning the foregoing matters, and death also, of another person, if the declarant was related to the other by blood, adoption, or marriage or was so intimately associated with the other's family as to be likely to have accurate information concerning the matter declared.

(5) [Transferred to Rule 807]

Source: (b)(5) added November 15, 1984, effective April 1, 1985; (b)(5) transferred to Rule 807 and (b)(5) comment added, effective January 1, 1999; (b)(3) and (b)(3) committee comment added and effective January 13, 2011.

Rule 805. Hearsay Within Hearsay

Hearsay included within hearsay is not excluded under the hearsay rule if each part of the combined statements conforms with an exception to the hearsay rule provided in these rules.

Rule 806. Attacking and Supporting Credibility of Declarant

When a hearsay statement, or a statement defined in Rule 801(d)(2)(C), (D), or (E), has been admitted in evidence, the credibility of the declarant may be attacked, and if attacked may be supported, by any evidence which would be admissible for those purposes if declarant had testified as a witness. Evidence of a statement or conduct by the declarant at any time, inconsistent with his hearsay statement, is not subject to any requirement that he may have been afforded an opportunity to deny or explain. If the party against whom a hearsay statement has been admitted calls the declarant as a witness, the party is entitled to examine him on the statement as if under cross-examination.

Rule 807. Residual Exception

A statement not specifically covered by Rule 803 or 804 but having equivalent circumstantial guarantees of trustworthiness, is not excluded by the hearsay rule, if the court determines that (A) the statement is offered as evidence of a material fact; (B) the statement is more probative on the point for which it is offered than any other evidence which the proponent can procure through reasonable efforts; and (C) the general purposes of these rules and the interests of justice will best be served by admission of the statement into evidence. However, a statement may not be admitted under this exception unless the proponent of it makes known to the adverse party sufficiently in advance of the trial or hearing to provide the adverse party with a fair opportunity to prepare to meet it, the proponent's intention to offer the statement and the particulars of it, including the name and address of the declarant.

Source: Entire rule amended and adopted November 25, 1998, effective January 1, 1999.

ARTICLE IX
AUTHENTICATION AND IDENTIFICATION

Rule 901. Requirement of Authentication or Identification

(a) **General provision.** The requirement of authentication or identification as a condition precedent to admissibility is satisfied by evidence sufficient to support a finding that the matter in question is what its proponent claims.

(b) **Illustrations.** By way of illustration only, and not by way of limitation, the following are examples of authentication or identification conforming with the requirements of this rule:

(1) **Testimony of witness with knowledge.** Testimony that a matter is what it is claimed to be.

(2) **Non-expert opinion on handwriting.** Non-expert opinion as to the genuineness of handwriting, based upon familiarity not acquired for purposes of the litigation.

(3) **Comparison by trier or expert witness.** Comparison by the trier of fact or by expert witnesses with specimens which have been authenticated.

(4) **Distinctive characteristics and the like.** Appearance, contents, substance, internal patterns,

or other distinctive characteristics, taken in conjunction with circumstances.

(5) **Voice identification.** Identification of a voice, whether heard firsthand or through mechanical or electronic transmission or recording, by opinion based upon hearing the voice at any time under circumstances connecting it with the alleged speaker.

(6) **Telephone conversations.** Telephone conversations, by evidence that a call was made to the number assigned at the time by the telephone company to a particular person or business, if (A) in the case of a person, circumstances, including self-identification, show the person answering to be the one called, or (B) in the case of business, the call was made to a place of business and the conversation related to business reasonably transacted over the telephone.

(7) **Public records or reports.** Evidence that a writing authorized by law to be recorded or filed and in fact recorded or filed in a public office, or a purported public record, report, statement, or data compilation, in any form, is from the public office where items of this nature are kept.

(8) **Ancient documents or data compilation.** Evidence that a document or data compilation, in any form, (A) is in such condition as to create no suspicion concerning its authenticity, (B) was in a

official capacity of an officer or employee of any entity included in paragraph (1) hereof, having no seal, if a public officer having a seal and having official duties in the district or political subdivision of the officer or employee certifies under seal that the signer has the official capacity and that the signature is genuine.

(3) **Foreign public documents.** A document purporting to be executed or attested in his official capacity by a person authorized by the laws of a foreign country to make the execution or attestation, and accompanied by a final certification as to the genuineness of signature and official position (A) of the executing or attesting person, or (B) of any foreign official whose certificate of genuineness of signature and official position relates to the execution or attestation or is in a chain of certificates of genuineness of signature and official position relating to the execution or attestation. A final certification may be made by a secretary of embassy or legation, consul general, consul, vice consul, or consular agent of the United States, or a diplomatic or consular official of the foreign country assigned or accredited to the United States. If reasonable opportunity has been given to all parties to investigate the authenticity and accuracy of official documents, the court may, for good cause shown, order that they be treated as presumptively authentic without final certification or permit them to be evidenced by an attested summary with or without final certification.

(4) **Certified copies of public records.** A copy of an official record or report or entry therein, or of a document authorized by law to be recorded or filed and actually recorded or filed in a public office, including data compilations in any form, certified as correct by the custodian or other person authorized to make the certification, by certificate complying with paragraph (1), (2), or (3) of this rule or complying with any Federal or Colorado Rule of Procedure, or with any Act of the United States Congress, or any statute of the State of Colorado.

(5) **Official publications.** Books, pamphlets, or other publications purporting to be issued by public authority.

(6) **Newspapers and periodicals.** Printed materials purporting to be newspapers or periodicals.

(7) **Trade inscriptions and the like.** Inscriptions, signs, tags, or labels purporting to have been affixed in the course of business and indicating ownership, control, or origin.

(8) **Acknowledged documents.** Documents accompanied by a certificate of acknowledgment executed in the manner provided by law by a notary public or other officer authorized by law to take acknowledgments.

(9) **Commercial paper and related documents.** Commercial paper, signatures thereon, and documents relating thereto to the extent provided by general commercial law.

(10) **Presumptions under legislative Act.** Any signature, document, or other matter declared by Act of the Congress of the United States, or by any statute of the State of Colorado to be presumptively or prima facie genuine or authentic.

(11) **Certified domestic record of regularly conducted activity.** The original or a duplicate of a domestic record of regularly conducted activity that would be admissible under Rule 803(6) if accompanied by an affidavit of its custodian or other qualified person, in a manner complying with any Colorado statute or rule prescribed by the Colorado Supreme Court, certifying that the record—

(a) was made at or near the time of the occurrence of the matters set forth by, or from information transmitted by, a person with knowledge of those matters;

(b) was kept in the course of the regularly conducted activity; and

(c) was made by the regularly conducted activity as a regular practice.

A party intending to offer a record into evidence under this paragraph must provide written notice of that intention to all adverse parties, and must make the record and affidavit available for inspection sufficiently in advance of their offer into evidence to provide an adverse party with a fair opportunity to challenge them.

(12) **Certified foreign records of regularly conducted activity.** In a civil case, the original or a duplicate of a foreign record of regularly conducted activity that would be admissible under rule 803(6) if accompanied by a written declaration by its custodian or other qualified person certifying that the record—

(a) was made at or near the time of the occurrence of the matters set forth by, or from information transmitted by, a person with knowledge of those matters;

(b) was kept in the course of the regularly conducted activity; and

(c) was made by the regularly conducted activity as a regular practice.

The declaration must be signed in a manner that, if falsely made, would subject the maker to criminal penalty under the laws of the country where the declaration is signed. A party intending to offer a record into evidence under this paragraph must provide written notice of that intention to all adverse parties, and must make the record and declaration available for inspection sufficiently in advance of their offer into evidence to provide an adverse party with a fair opportunity to challenge them.

Source: (11) and (12) added and adopted June 20, 2002, effective July 1, 2002.

Rule 903. Subscribing Witness's Testimony Unnecessary

The testimony of a subscribing witness is not necessary to authenticate a writing unless required by the laws of the jurisdiction whose laws govern the validity of the writing.

ARTICLE X
CONTENTS OF WRITINGS, RECORDINGS, AND PHOTOGRAPHS

Rule 1001. Definitions

For purposes of this article the following definitions are applicable:

(1) **Writings and recordings.** "Writings" and "recordings" consist of letters, words, or numbers, or their equivalent, set down by handwriting, typewriting, printing, photostating, photographing, magnetic impulse, mechanical or electronic recording, or other form of data compilation.

(2) **Photographs.** "Photographs" include still photographs, X-ray films, videotapes, and motion pictures.

(3) **Original.** An "original" of a writing or recording is the writing or recording itself or any counterpart intended to have the same effect by a person executing or issuing it. An "original" of a photograph includes the negative or any print therefrom. If data are stored in a computer or similar device, any printout or other output readable by sight, shown to reflect the data accurately, is an "original."

(4) **Duplicate.** A "duplicate" is a counterpart produced by the same impression as the original, or from

the same matrix, or by means of photography, including enlargements and miniatures, or by mechanical or electronic re-recording, or by chemical reproduction, or by other equivalent techniques which accurately reproduce the original.

Rule 1002. Requirement of Original

To prove the content of a writing, recording, or photograph, the original writing, recording, or photograph is required, except as otherwise provided in these rules or by statute of the State of Colorado or of the United States.

Rule 1003. Admissibility of Duplicates

A duplicate is admissible to the same extent as an original unless (1) a genuine question is raised as to the authenticity of the original or (2) in the circumstances it would be unfair to admit the duplicate in lieu of the original.

Rule 1004. Admissibility of Other Evidence of Contents

The original is not required, and other evidence of the contents of a writing, recording, or photograph is admissible if:

(1) **Originals lost or destroyed.** All originals are lost or have been destroyed, unless the proponent lost or destroyed them in bad faith; or

(2) **Original not obtainable.** No original can be obtained by any available judicial process or procedure; or

(3) **Original in possession of opponent.** At a time when an original was under the control of the party against whom offered, he was put on notice, by the pleadings or otherwise, that the contents would be a subject of proof at the hearing, and he does not produce the original at the hearing; or

(4) **Collateral matters.** The writing, recording, or photograph is not closely related to a controlling issue.

Rule 1005. Public Records

The contents of an official record, or of a document authorized to be recorded, or filed and actually recorded or filed, including data compilations in any form, if otherwise admissible, may be proved by copy, certified as correct in accordance with Rule 902 or testified to be correct by a witness who has compared it with the original. If a copy which complies with the foregoing cannot be obtained by the exercise of reasonable diligence, then other evidence of the contents may be given.

Rule 1006. Summaries

The contents of voluminous writings, recordings, or photographs which cannot conveniently be examined in court may be presented in the form of a chart, summary, or calculation. The originals or duplicates shall be made available for examination or copying, or both, by other parties at reasonable time and place. The court may order that they be produced in court.

Rule 1007. Testimony or Written Admission of Party

Contents of writings, recordings, or photographs may be proved by the testimony or deposition of the party against whom offered or by his written admission, without accounting for the non-production of the original.

Rule 1008. Functions of Court and Jury

When the admissibility of other evidence of contents of writings, recordings, or photographs under these rules depends upon the fulfillment of a condition of fact, the question whether the condition has been fulfilled is ordinarily for the court to determine in accordance with the provisions of Rule 104. However, when an issue is raised (a) whether the asserted writing ever existed, or (b) whether another writing, recording, or photograph produced at the trial is the original, or (c) whether other evidence of contents correctly reflects the contents, the issue is for the trier of fact to determine as in the case of other issues of fact.

ARTICLE XI
MISCELLANEOUS RULES

Rule 1101. Applicability of Rules

(a) **Courts.** These rules apply to all courts in the State of Colorado.

(b) **Proceedings generally.** These rules apply generally to civil actions, to criminal proceedings, and to contempt proceedings, except those in which the court may act summarily.

(c) **Rule of privilege.** The rule with respect to privileges applies at all stages of all actions, cases, and proceedings.

(d) **Rules inapplicable.** The rules (other than with respect to privileges) do not apply in the following situations:

(1) **Preliminary questions of fact.** The determination of questions of fact preliminary to admissibility of evidence when the issue is to be determined by the court under Rule 104.

(2) **Grand jury.** Proceedings before grand juries.

(3) **Miscellaneous proceedings.** Proceedings for extradition or rendition; preliminary examinations in criminal cases; sentencing, or granting or revoking probation; issuance of warrants for arrest, criminal

summonses, and search warrants; and proceedings with respect to release on bail or otherwise.

(e) **Rules applicable in part.** In any special statutory proceedings, these rules apply to the extent that matters of evidence are not provided for in the statutes which govern procedure therein.

Rule 1102. (No Colorado Rule Codified)

Rule 1103. Title

These rules shall be known and cited as the Colorado Rules of Evidence, or CRE.